Analogies 3

- Problem-Solving Strategies
- Exercises for Analysis
- Vocabulary Study

Arthur Liebman

School Specialty, Inc.
Cambridge and Toronto

ABOUT THE AUTHOR

Arthur Liebman, Ph.D., author and editor of more then a dozen books ranging on subjects from Shakespeare to Sherlock Holmes, has taught English on all levels from middle school through graduate school. A recognized expert on college preparatory material, his teaching experience includes more the twenty years of SAT review classes. His most recent publications for high schoolers are *English Elements 1 and 2*, worktexts on critical reading, vocabulary study, verbal reasoning, grammar for writing and speaking, and standard English usage. Dr. Liebman is currently a faculty member at New York University, where he teaches humanities and world literature; and a lecturer on drama and mystery fiction at the New School for Social Research.

In addition to his teaching and writing, Dr. Liebman has been a featured speaker at conventions of the National Council of Teachers of English and a consultant for the New York State Board of Regents in the preparation of the state-wide comprehensive English examinations. In collaboration with his wife Joyce Anne Liebman, concert pianist and composer, he has been author and lyricist of a number of musicals for school and community theatre.

Printed in Benton Harbor, MI, in December 2014
ISBN 978-0-8388-2229-6

12 13 14 15 PPG 16 15 14

CONTENTS

TO THE TEACHER

Analogies 3 is a three-part worktext. While its central purpose is to offer practice in solving analogy problems, it also offers students an opportunity to expand their vocabularies.

Part 1 of this book consists of instructional material on strategies for solving analogy problems. Part 2 presents four groups of analogy exercises, with each group comprised of one hundred items. For manageable practice, each of these groups is subdivided into five units of twenty items each. Part 3 contains four vocabulary groups of one hundred words each, with the defined and alphabetized words representing some of the most difficult words in the corresponding analogy group. These vocabulary entries may be studied before doing the analogies as preparation for more successful work with them, or they can be used as reference material during or after work on the analogies.

Additional practice on analogy problem solving and on the vocabulary contained in this worktext is available in *Analogies 3: 8 Vocabulary and 4 Analogy Quizzes*, a booklet of perforated pages. Permission is granted to reproduce these quizzes for use with *Analogies 3*.

TO THE STUDENT

The analogy questions on the SAT 1 are designed to test your higher-level thinking skills. By requiring you to demonstrate an ability to see the relationship between two given words or terms, the analogy section of the test attempts to fathom your power to reason and your ability to see the relationship between given facts and ideas. This ability to see complex relationships is regarded by all educators as a basic factor in intellectual development.

The analogy question is the most frequently asked question on standardized exams. Junior high school students encounter analogies for admission to select high schools; senior high school students encounter analogies on college admission tests. Even college graduates are required to solve analogies on the difficult tests that are devised for admission to graduate schools of medicine, law, accounting and other professional fields. Thus, it is safe to say that sooner or later your ability to solve analogies will be an important factor in your educational success.

This book is designed to explain the various techniques of answering analogy questions. Carefully read the introductory material in "Analogies: How to Solve Them." It's written in clear conversational English with a minimum of technical terms. You should be able to master easily the direct, step-by-step approach that it presents. After you've grasped the basics of analogy solving, go on to the various analogy drills.

Don't be discouraged if you have difficulty at first. Keep at it. Continue to work diligently, and you will soon master even elusive analogies; then you'll be certain to score well on this important section of your SAT 1.

In conclusion, we would like to remind you—in the form of an analogy —that

**Effort leads to success
as study leads to high scores.**

THE BRIDGE-SENTENCE

The key to all analogy questions is to understand clearly the relationship between two given words. The best way to do this is to make up a simple statement using the two words as they relate to each other. We will call this sentence a bridge-sentence because it clearly connects the two words.

Let's consider this example:

   HILARIOUS : AMUSING

This relationship may be stated as

   Hilarious is greater than amusing.

Or you may state it as

   Amusing is not as strong as hilarious.

or even

   Hilarious is more fun than amusing.

Any of these will do. Don't worry about the correct English of your bridge-sentence. You are the only one who has to understand it, and you do not have to maintain the standards you would in a formal paper.

Now let's try a few more.

1. TREE : FOREST   *A tree is in a forest.*
   A forest has a tree.

2. WATER : PIPE   *Water goes through a pipe.*
   A pipe carries water.

3. ANGER : RAGE   *Anger is weaker than rage.*
   Rage is stronger than anger.

4. COLOR : RAINBOW   *Color is part of a rainbow.*
   A rainbow has color.

5. BALLOON : BASKETBALL   *A balloon is shaped like a basketball.*
   A basketball looks like a balloon.

6. FREIGHTER : VESSEL   *A freighter is a kind of vessel.*
   A vessel can be a freighter.

THE ANALOGY PROBLEM

An analogy problem presents one pair of key words followed by a listing of pairs of other words. The relationship between one pair of words in this listing will be the same as or similar to the relationship between the pair of key words.

Here's an example:

   MONEY : POCKET ::
   a. grass : lawn
   b. prisoner : court
   c. safe : jewels
   d. towel : laundromat
   e. books : library

1

To solve this analogy problem, you must find the one pair, from among those in *a* through *e*, in which the words relate to each other in the same way that *money* does to *pocket*. Begin by composing a bridge-sentence. Then mentally insert each of the five choices into your bridge-sentence; the correct answer should fit it perfectly. Remember, if you use the second word of the key pair <u>first</u> in your bridge-sentence, you must also use the second word of each possible answer pair first when you are fitting it into your bridge-sentence. When making a good bridge-sentence to solve an analogy, you can never make a word-order mistake.

Bridge-sentence—*Money is kept in a pocket.*

    a. *Grass is kept on a lawn.*
      (No. Grass grows on a lawn.)

    b. *A prisoner is kept in a court.*
      (No. A prisoner is tried in a court.)

    c. *A safe is kept in jewels.*
      (No. Wrong word order; does not fit your bridge-sentence.)

    d. *A towel is kept in a laundromat.*
      (No. A towel is cleaned in a laundromat; it is usually kept in a linen closet.)

    e. *Books are kept in a library.*
      (Yes. This statement is true. Right word order.)

Correct answer: (e) books : library

Now you're ready to try another:

    HUMORIST : WITTY ::
    a. soldier : daring
    b. fanatic : murderous
    c. manager : autocratic
    d. Amazon : strong
    e. motorist : alert

Construct your bridge-sentence with the two capitalized key words before looking at the choices.

Bridge-sentence—*A humorist is a witty person.*

    a. *A soldier is a daring person.*
      (But some soldiers are not daring; some may be cowards.)

    b. *A fanatic is a murderous person.*
      (But many sports fans, music lovers, or enthusiastic gardeners may be regarded as fanatics, but they are <u>not</u> murderous.)

    c. *A manager is an autocratic person.*
      (But many managers are not autocratic. They may consider their staffs, consult with their employees, etc.)

    d. *An Amazon is a strong person.*
      (Sounds right. All Amazons are strong, as all humorists are witty. Save this choice, but check all the possibilities; never make a final decision until you've considered all five choices.)

    e. *A motorist is an alert person.*
      (Unfortunately some motorists are not alert; many accidents are caused by drivers who are not alert.)

Correct answer: (d) Amazon : strong.

PRACTICE BRIDGE-SENTENCES

Make up two clear bridge-sentences for each of the following pairs.

1. JUSTICE : JUDGE

   _____

   _____

2. NAIL : HAMMER

   _____

   _____

3. SPEED : SPRINT

   _____

   _____

4. ENVY : FAME

   _____

   _____

5. ARTIST : STUDIO

   _____

   _____

6. THUMB : HAND

   _____

   _____

7. GIFT : BENEFACTOR

   _____

   _____

8. APPLAUSE : PERFORMER

   _____

   _____

9. EPIC : LENGTHY

   _____

   _____

10. CITADEL : DEFENSE

   _____

   _____

WORDS WITH MORE THAN ONE MEANING

Be careful of an analogy where a word may have more than one meaning because it can be more than one part of speech. In such a case, determine whether the word is used as an adjective, verb, or noun.

Let's try a tricky one.

> INSTITUTE : BEGIN ::
> a. finish : final
> b. memorize : educate
> c. exercise : muscle
> d. ripple : wave
> e. assault : attack

Institute as a noun may be defined as *an organization or society formed for a special purpose.* However, as a verb, *institute* means *to begin.* After deciding to use *institute* as a verb meaning *to begin,* you are ready to construct your bridge-sentence.

> *Institute is the same as begin.*

> a. *Finish is the same as final.*
> (Might sound right at first, but there's a problem with this choice. *Final* is either an adjective or a noun, and you are using *institute* as a verb. Therefore, *finish* and *final* are not the same as *institute* and *begin.*)

> b. *Study is the same as educate.*
> (Incorrect because when one studies, one acquires knowledge; whereas, when one educates, one usually transmits knowledge. Studying and educating are not always the same kinds of processes.)

> c. *Exercise is the same as muscle.*
> (Incorrect. Muscle may develop as a result of exercise, but the two are not the same—and muscle is a noun, not a verb.)

> d. *Ripple is the same as wave.*
> (Incorrect. To ripple is to form little waves. Plus, none of the meanings of the verb *wave* is the same as the verb *ripple.*)

> e. *Assault is the same as attack.*
> (Correct. This pair of words fits the bridge-sentence very well. Both of these verbs are the same, just as both verbs in the bridge-sentence are the same.)

For additional practice, look at some more words that have more than one meaning. All of the words on the next page fall into this category.

Each of the following words can have more than one meaning. For each word, give two different meanings and indicate the part of speech of each.

1. HARBOR   a) _____

                b) _____

2. AIR   a) _____

                b) _____

3. ATTRIBUTE   a) _____

                b) _____

4. FLOWER   a) _____

                b) _____

5. TABLE   a) _____

                b) _____

6. INITIAL   a) _____

                b) _____

7. CHAMPION   a) _____

                b) _____

8. CONTENT   a) _____

                b) _____

9. CONTRACT   a) _____

                b) _____

10. COUPLE   a) _____

                b) _____

11. FUEL   a) _____

                b) _____

12. HUSBAND   a) _____

                b) _____

13. RENEGADE   a) _____

                b) _____

14. REFUSE   a) _____

                b) _____

15. UNIFORM   a) _____

                b) _____

TWO-STEP ANALOGIES

Sometimes an analogy will contain two or more pairs that seem to fit your bridge-sentence. In fact, many of the analogies on the SAT 1 require you to take a second step before making your final choice.

Let's practice a tricky analogy in which a number of choices seems to be correct. Then let's take the second step and make the right choice.

BOOK : CHAPTERS ::
a. column : figures
b. summary : facts
c. census : data
d. deck : cards
e. poem : stanzas

Step 1

Bridge-sentence—*A book is made up of chapters.*

a. *A column is made up of figures.*
(But a column may also be made up of words, phrases, numbers. Incorrect.)

b. *A summary is made up of facts.*
(But a summary may be made up of many things—details, paragraphs, etc. Incorrect.)

c. *A census is made up of data.*
(Seems to be a possibility; let's save it and consider it again after we've tried the rest of the choices. Possible.)

d. *A deck is made up of cards.*
(Seems to be correct; save it. Let's try the last choice.)

e. *A poem is made up of stanzas.*
(Seems to be correct too. Possible.)

Step 2

Step 2 involves taking a closer look. You must now ask yourself which of the remaining possible choices comes closest to the original. One way to do this is to think about subject matter and find the pair that deals with the same thing as the original pair.

Let's refine the bridge-sentence to say: *A book is a literary work divided into chapters.* The answer to the analogy problem soon becomes apparent because, of the three possibilities—(c), (d), and (e)—only (e) contains literary terms: *A poem is a literary work divided into stanzas.* The correct answer, then, is (e).

Now let's try another:

ALLY : ENEMY ::
a. companion : colleague
b. friend : foe
c. black : white
d. acceptance : approval
e. partner : boss

Step 1: Compose a bridge-sentence—*An ally is the opposite of an enemy.*

    a. *A companion is the opposite of a colleague.*
       (A colleague is an associate or co-worker. Incorrect.)

    b. *Friend is the opposite of foe.*
       (Sounds correct; save it and read the remaining choices.)

    c. *Black is the opposite of white.*
       (Sounds correct also. Save it for reconsideration.)

    d. *Acceptance is the opposite of approval.*
       (Acceptance usually follows approval. Incorrect.)

    e. *A partner is the opposite of a boss.*
       (A partner often shares authority; a partner often acts as a boss. Incorrect.)

Step 2: Compare the two analogies that fit the bridge-sentence; keep in mind that both terms in the bridge-sentence relate to strife or fighting.

    c. *Black is the opposite of white*, but this relationship has nothing to do with strife or fighting. Incorrect.

    b. *Friend is the opposite of foe*, and this pair refers to strife or fighting, as do the key words. Correct.

Step 2 shows that your final choice is (b) friend : foe.

ANALOGIES—THE TOP TEN TYPES

Being aware of the most frequently asked analogy types will give you a much better chance of mastering analogies. Study this list of the ten types of analogies that are most frequently asked on standardized tests like the SAT 1. Keep them in mind as you construct your bridge-sentences. They will help you find the right answers.

1. WORD : SYNONYM
   scent : aroma
   magazine : periodical

2. WORD : ANTONYM
   destroy : build
   remember : forget

3. CAUSE : EFFECT
   microbe : disease
   cloud : rain

4. PART : WHOLE
   leg : body
   branch : tree

5. CONDITION : LESSER DEGREE OF THE SAME CONDITION
   flooded : moist
   dark : murky

6. CONDITION : GREATER DEGREE OF THE SAME CONDITION
   intelligent : brilliant
   bright : radiant

7. PERSON OR THING : CHARACTERISTIC OR QUALITY
   teacher : scholarly
   hero : brave

8. PERSON OR THING : GROUP OR CATEGORY
   accountant : professional
   hammer : tool

9. PERSON OR THING : ACTION OR FUNCTION
   actor : portray
   knife : cut

10. WORKER : DEVICE HE/SHE USES
    mechanic : wrench
    surgeon : scalpel

ANALOGIES—THE SECONDARY SIX TYPES

The following types of analogies may appear on the SAT 1 but are not as common as the top ten types.

1. SCIENCE : SUBJECT OF SCIENCE
   anthropology : humankind
   botany : plants

2. GENDER QUESTIONS
   colt : filly
   stallion : mare

3. SYMBOL : BUSINESS, GOVERNMENT, RELIGION
   flag : country
   cross : Christianity

4. FAMILY RELATIONSHIP
   mother : daughter
   uncle : niece

*5. GRAMMATICAL RELATIONSHIP
   I : me
   we : us

*6. GENERAL KNOWLEDGE
   Shakespeare : Hamlet
   Twain : Tom Sawyer

Now that you've read the preceding instructional material carefully, it's time to do the analogy exercises. You will see that each group of analogies begins with the easiest ones and ends with the most difficult. Thus, you should find the first groups easy, the middle groups a bit tricky, and the last groups very difficult.

Work carefully, keep trying, and don't get discouraged. Keep at it, and you'll soon master "those tricky analogies."

---

*This kind of analogy appears very rarely.

UNIT A

Directions: Select the pair of words that most nearly expresses the relationship of the pair of key words given in capital letters. Circle the letter preceding the pair you choose.

1. HORSE : REINS : :
   a. bird : migration
   b. anarchist : government
   c. greyhound : track
   d. citizen : law
   e. diplomat : negotiations

2. WHEEL : RIM : :
   a. tie : pin
   b. hat : band
   c. shirt : sleeve
   d. tire : spoke
   e. property : fence

3. AWNING : SUN : :
   a. veil : face
   b. mask : eyes
   c. netting : mosquitos
   d. antennae : television
   e. dam : fish

4. SKYSCRAPER : FRAMEWORK : :
   a. web : spider
   b. cloth : strand
   c. net : string
   d. restaurant : menu
   e. body : skeleton

5. DEATH : PESTILENCE : :
   a. destruction : war
   b. lava : eruption
   c. appetite : hunger
   d. tremor : earthquake
   e. hysteria : fever

6. HERO : INTREPID : :
   a. defender : potent
   b. champion : admired
   c. gargoyle : mythical
   d. soldier : valorous
   e. coward : fearful

7. PATRIOT : JINGOIST : :
   a. enthusiast : zealot
   b. student : teacher
   c. veteran : novice
   d. braggart : liar
   e. prodigy : prodigal

8. SINFUL : VIRTUOUS : :
   a. lethargic : sluggish
   b. arduous : romantic
   c. abstemious : indulgent
   d. nefarious : honorable
   e. exorbitant : expensive

9. SUPERFICIAL : CURSORY : :
   a. moderate : destructive
   b. enthralling : repulsive
   c. copious : scant
   d. injurious : deleterious
   e. dissent : admission

10. WEAKEN : SUCCUMB : :
    a. grow : thrive
    b. sleep : slumber
    c. persist : relent
    d. ask : query
    e. melt : disintegrate

11. GHOST : ETHEREAL : :
    a. torso : small
    b. spectre : occult
    c. statue : bronze
    d. personality : neurotic
    e. vision : illusionary

12. LOVER : ARDENT : :
    a. sluggard : lazy
    b. steward : odious
    c. parent : wise
    d. judge : capricious
    e. sentry : hostile

13. CADAVER : PERSON : :
    a. corpse : ghost
    b. carcass : beast
    c. relic : symbol
    d. pelvis : body
    e. life : death

14. PUZZLE : ENIGMA : :
    a. valedictorian : champion
    b. religious : ecclesiastic
    c. chronic : malady
    d. mystery : secret
    e. ordnance : law

15. INIQUITOUS : VILLAIN : :
    a. frivolous : monk
    b. instantaneous : enigma
    c. intrepid : explorer
    d. religious : cathedral
    e. altruistic : mercenary

16. FETID : STENCH : :
    a. translucent : light
    b. muted : noise
    c. besotted : decoration
    d. pungent : odor
    e. strident : sound

17. PRUDENCE : CAUTION : :
    a. pulchritude : treachery
    b. innuendo : privacy
    c. aversion : interest
    d. valor : energy
    e. fealty : allegiance

18. GOURMAND : GOBBLE : :
    a. epicure : examine
    b. gourmet : chew
    c. expert : reflect
    d. proletarian : drink
    e. host : entertain

19. COMPASSIONATE : MERCIFUL : :
    a. flamboyant : subdued
    b. doctor : patient
    c. ruthless : lenient
    d. frugal : thrifty
    e. benevolent : charitable

20. FORENSIC : ARGUMENTATIVE : :
    a. elliptical : considerate
    b. nebulous : aggravating
    c. deciduous : annual
    d. altruistic : unselfish
    e. concise : verbose

UNIT B

Directions: Select the pair of words that most nearly expresses the relationship of the pair of key words in capital letters. Circle the letter preceding the pair you choose.

1. MOUNTAIN : VALLEY : :
   a. hill : river
   b. mound : plain
   c. cliff : gorge
   d. pinnacle : peak
   e. cloud : plateau

2. BANQUET : MEAL : :
   a. boulder : bulwark
   b. fiasco : defeat
   c. colt : stallion
   d. debacle : deluge
   e. battle : war

3. GIRDER : STEEL : :
   a. spool : thread
   b. brick : stone
   c. marrow : bone
   d. shoe : leather
   e. plank : wood

4. CENTURY : DECADE : :
   a. quarter : nickel
   b. millenium : era
   c. dollar : dime
   d. thermometer : degree
   e. year : month

5. ALPHABET : LETTERS : :
   a. wardrobe : dresses
   b. lexicon : letters
   c. code : secrets
   d. spectrum : colors
   e. beach : bathers

6. PAW : TOE : :
   a. beak : nose
   b. thumb : hand
   c. heart : organ
   d. knee : joint
   e. talon : nail

7. BURN : SCORCH : :
   a. old : unfashionable
   b. hot : warm
   c. water : pour
   d. dull : polish
   e. brillance : shine

8. EMINENT : RENOWNED : :
   a. veteran : recruit
   b. deranged : insane
   c. obscure : distinguished
   d. cynical : witty
   e. celebrated : illustrious

9. MULL : CONSIDER : :
   a. reflect : think
   b. hesitate : act
   c. doze : nap
   d. shake : shudder
   e. mirror : light

10. ALLURING : CAPTIVATING : :
    a. reluctant : unwilling
    b. contrite : sad
    c. crass : uncouth
    d. charming : winsome
    e. obnoxious : fascinating

11. CORDIAL : HOSPITABLE : :
    a. amiable : genial
    b. dexterous : skillful
    c. hostile : sociable
    d. hilarious : amusing
    e. host : guest

12. BLUNT : CANDID : :
    a. affirm : deny
    b. aggrieved : sad
    c. reticent : outspoken
    d. forthright : frank
    e. reporter : author

13. ENTHUSIASTIC : FERVENT : :
    a. rustic : bucolic
    b. ardent : zealous
    c. benign : generous
    d. apathetic : intense
    e. salesperson : customer

14. DEPRESSED : DOWNCAST : :
    a. brusque : polite
    b. carefree : glum
    c. carping : complaining
    d. victor : loser
    e. crestfallen : dejected

15. MINX : PRUDE : :
    a. soldier : veteran
    b. champion : contender
    c. radical : conservative
    d. new : old
    e. student : graduate

16. MORTIFIED : HUMILIATED : :
    a. victim : bully
    b. canny : shrewd
    c. badgered : bothered
    d. captivating : charming
    e. ashamed : chagrined

17. UNCULTIVATED : FALLOW : :
    a. fertile : arid
    b. exact : punctilious
    c. nebulous : clear
    d. precise : original
    e. incognito : famous

18. GREEDY : RAPACIOUS : :
    a. grasping : strong
    b. altruistic : benevolent
    c. egotistic : confident
    d. munificent : gentle
    e. insurgent : orderly

19. ACRIMONIOUS : DEBATE : :
    a. reasonable : appointment
    b. harmonious : conversation
    c. brief : limerick
    d. logical : editorial
    e. vituperative : argument

20. QUIBBLE : CAVIL : :
    a. rationalize : divide
    b. proclaim : triumph
    c. enjoin : order
    d. demur : release
    e. recant : sing

UNIT C

Directions: Select the pair of words that most nearly expresses the relationship of the pair of key words in capital letters. Circle the letter preceding the pair you choose.

1. MINISTER : CLERGY : :
   a. philosopher : concept
   b. senator : legislature
   c. scholar : curriculum
   d. prosecutor : courtroom
   e. author : literature

2. ARSENAL : GUNS : :
   a. asylum : doctors
   b. chain : links
   c. fortress : defense
   d. catalog : information
   e. library : books

3. WHEEL : POTTER : :
   a. chisel : prisoner
   b. trowel : hunter
   c. scalpel : surgeon
   d. trident : tribune
   e. shoe : cobbler

4. SPIDER : WEB : :
   a. carpenter : house
   b. bird : nest
   c. eskimo : igloo
   d. beaver : bevy
   e. bee : aviary

5. HYMN : SONG : :
   a. refrain : rendition
   b. dirge : march
   c. choral : chorus
   d. liturgy : routine
   e. priest : congregation

6. PRESSURE : ALLEVIATE : :
   a. stress : emphasize
   b. affluence : increase
   c. tension : reduce
   d. influence : expand
   e. size : diminish

7. PUNISH : CASTIGATE : :
   a. censure : reject
   b. laud : praise
   c. instill : engender
   d. facilitate : obstruct
   e. adulate : enhance

8. REFUTE : CORROBORATE : :
   a. surpass : excel
   b. allay : cooperate
   c. amend : precede
   d. vocation : hobby
   e. disagree : substantiate

9. MENTOR : STUDENT : :
   a. accountant : record
   b. colleague : college
   c. prophet : prediction
   d. consultant : business
   e. minister : congregant

10. AFFLUENT : PAUPER : :
    a. destitute : bankrupt
    b. dauntless : coward
    c. viaduct : bridge
    d. agrarian : farmer
    e. stadium : diamond

11. INACTIVE : STATIC : :
    a. tumultuous : quiet
    b. archaic : modern
    c. disorganized : chaotic
    d. venemous : laconic
    e. banal : original

12. SYMPOSIUM : FORUM : :
    a. corroboration : meeting
    b. collation : innundation
    c. soiree : party
    d. debut : audience
    e. bunch : pack

13. BULLY : BELLICOSE : :
    a. miser : avaricious
    b. monarch : perceptive
    c. despot : munificent
    d. protagonist : abstruse
    e. buffoon : powerful

14. TRANSITORY : EPHEMERAL : :
    a. indigenous : poor
    b. ecclesiastical : religious
    c. burnished : tarnished
    d. renovated : constructed
    e. alienate : immigrate

15. GUILT : LADEN : :
    a. hilarity : encompassed
    b. ribbons : bedecked
    c. water : saturated
    d. danger : fraught
    e. taste : decorated

16. BENIGN : MALIGNANT : :
    a. gentle : menacing
    b. subtle : covert
    c. flagrant : bold
    d. subdued : silent
    e. slow : swift

17. STYLUS : PEN : :
    a. awl : knife
    b. crayon : pencil
    c. coil : chain
    d. hammer : nail
    e. paper : cardboard

18. CONGENIALITY : FRIENDSHIP : :
    a. depression : sadness
    b. gaudiness : bravery
    c. determination : success
    d. felicity : happiness
    e. meditation : knowledge

19. PISCATORIAL : FISH : :
    a. tonsorial : hair
    b. gastronomic : strength
    c. pliable : teeth
    d. corporal : death
    e. tutorial : class

20. WASTREL : PARSIMONIOUS : :
    a. spendthrift : stingy
    b. event : propitious
    c. fanatic : rabid
    d. hiker : sedentary
    e. mendicant : destitute

UNIT D

Directions: Select the pair of words that most nearly expresses the relationship of the pair of key words in capital letters. Circle the letter preceding the pair you choose.

1. DIRECTOR : MOVIE : :
   a. coach : campus
   b. manager : business
   c. author : fiction
   d. mother : family
   e. driver : wheel

2. RIVET : STEEL : :
   a. bullet : wall
   b. stitch : cloth
   c. cement : brick
   d. nail : wood
   e. mortar : brick

3. CLOTH : SWATCH : :
   a. rug : mat
   b. foot : inch
   c. shoe : lace
   d. imagination : figment
   e. wood : splinter

4. VOTER : ELECTORATE : :
   a. militia : military
   b. minister : clergy
   c. priest : laity
   d. senator : constituency
   e. queen : regency

5. COLLATE : PAGES : :
   a. design : projects
   b. comprehend : data
   c. alphabetize : words
   d. organize : workers
   e. conceive : ideas

6. KNELL : BELL : :
   a. thud : chime
   b. tinkle : gong
   c. roar : radar
   d. squeak : board
   e. boom : cannon

7. BLISSFUL : ECSTATIC : :
   a. bride : marriage
   b. fickle : changeable
   c. feasible : practical
   d. elated : jubilant
   e. despondent : joyous

8. QUARREL : ENEMIES : :
   a. discord : allies
   b. affection : clients
   c. discourse : friends
   d. dissipation : resources
   e. persiflage : adversaries

9. TRIVIAL : MONUMENTAL : :
   a. elementary : basic
   b. simple : ingenious
   c. altruistic : philanthropic
   d. voluminous : copious
   e. stipend : compensation

10. VOLT : ELECTRICITY : :
    a. decibel : sound
    b. volume : noise
    c. bulb : wire
    d. amp : weight
    e. tone : music

11. AMENDMENT : CONSTITUTION : :
    a. postscript : paragraph
    b. rider : bill
    c. sentence : period
    d. overture : opera
    e. epilogue : prelude

12. EXTORT : MONEY : :
    a. evoke : response
    b. placate : foe
    c. conjure : dream
    d. satiate : desire
    e. stigmatize : reputation

13. PAROCHIAL : NARROW : :
    a. urbane : opaque
    b. cosmopolitan : broad
    c. arid : moist
    d. austere : frivolous
    e. brawny : weak

14. GURU : WISDOM : :
    a. scholar : research
    b. prodigy : youth
    c. genius : talent
    d. wastrel : wealth
    e. youth : foolishness

15. APATHETIC : ENTHUSIASTIC : :
    a. cadaverous : perceptive
    b. acrimonious : hateful
    c. gullible : suspicious
    d. piquant : aromatic
    e. tethered : active

16. THESPIAN : THEATRE : :
    a. novice : boulevard
    b. virtuoso : cathedral
    c. veteran : battle
    d. pedagogue : school
    e. patrician : shop

17. BOVINE : COW : :
    a. canine : cat
    b. piscine : elephant
    c. ursine : bear
    d. vulpine : cat
    e. assinine : mule

18. FLUSTERED : CONFUSED : :
    a. secular : religious
    b. imperturbable : calm
    c. sedulous : selective
    d. meticulous : brazen
    e. succulent : distasteful

19. AMBIGUOUS : CLEAR : :
    a. inanimate : lifeless
    b. adroit : skillful
    c. recondite : incomprehensible
    d. virulent : bitter
    e. generous : niggardly

20. PALADIN : CHAMPION : :
    a. philanthropist : pauper
    b. talisman : giant
    c. scapegoat : pet
    d. solon : legislator
    e. plebiscite : survey

UNIT E

Directions: Select the pair of words that most nearly expresses the relationship of the pair of key words in capital letters. Circle the letter preceding the pair you choose.

1. MILE : LAND : :
   a. watt : air
   b. kilometer : yard
   c. acre : soil
   d. quadrangle : square
   e. knot : water

2. FOREMAN : BOSS : :
   a. queen : king
   b. student : teacher
   c. employee : colleague
   d. admiral : general
   e. department : manager

3. ARCHIPELAGO : ISLAND : :
   a. aisle : carpet
   b. sandwich : ham
   c. ocean : water
   d. landscape : mountain
   e. constellation : star

4. ACTRESS : REPERTOIRE : :
   a. sailor : chart
   b. teacher : students
   c. restauranteur : menu
   d. dancer : talent
   e. comet : orbit

5. PARABLE : FABLE : :
   a. author : novel
   b. myth : humankind
   c. legend : fact
   d. school : classroom
   e. anecdote : story

6. CHILD : ADOLESCENT : :
   a. ancestor : heir
   b. whelp : puppy
   c. fledgling : adult
   d. prelate : clergyperson
   e. tadpole : frog

7. ALIAS : CRIMINAL : :
   a. epithet : name
   b. hyperbole : politician
   c. muse : poet
   d. pseudonym : author
   e. byline : journalist

8. PARTNER : COLLABORATE : :
   a. sponsor : admire
   b. patron : detest
   c. challenger : fear
   d. colleague : confer
   e. protagonist : revere

9. BENEFACTOR : AID : :
   a. harbinger : foreshadow
   b. citizen : vote
   c. Samaritan : rescue
   d. mime : motion
   e. conqueror : administer

10. SAND : DUNE : :
    a. pebbles : boulder
    b. trees : copse
    c. ripples : water
    d. pennies : dime
    e. concrete : building

11. DANCE : TANGO : :
    a. opera : libretto
    b. volume : dictionary
    c. concert : singer
    d. ballet : dancer
    e. song : madrigal

12. REWARD : PRAISE : :
    a. denounce : repay
    b. chastise : forgive
    c. rebuke : insult
    d. punish : castigate
    e. debit : destroy

13. BURGEON : DIMINISH : :
    a. refresh : renew
    b. discard : reject
    c. satisfy : accept
    d. scamper : stroll
    e. flourish : wither

14. LICENSE : DRIVER : :
    a. badge : authority
    b. telegram : messenger
    c. commission : officer
    d. diploma : student
    e. mandate : candidate

15. ANXIOUS : APPREHENSIVE : :
    a. fortuitous : accidental
    b. criminal : justice
    c. imminent : famous
    d. uneasy : perturbed
    e. unruffled : troubled

16. GULLIBLE : YOUTHFUL : :
    a. martial : infantile
    b. morose : thoughtless
    c. sophisticated : mature
    d. jocose : childish
    e. eminent : elderly

17. DISGRUNTLED : LOSER : :
    a. evoked : apprentice
    b. superior : victor
    c. cloistered : sage
    d. convened : wastrel
    e. duped : fool

18. QUIXOTIC : PRACTICAL : :
    a. loquacious : taciturn
    b. myopic : accurate
    c. chimerical : viable
    d. quintessential : significance
    e. truculent : docile

19. DAUNTLESS : VALIANT : :
    a. plaintiff : witness
    b. heedless : thoughtful
    c. timorous : practical
    d. heinous : admirable
    e. plucky : courageous

20. CAPTIOUS : APPRECIATIVE : :
    a. Herculean : puny
    b. mordant : deceased
    c. covetous : agreeable
    d. despondent : cheerful
    e. chanting : complaining

UNIT F

Directions: Select the pair of words that most nearly expresses the relationship of the pair of key words in capital letters. Circle the letter preceding the pair you choose.

1. THIMBLE : FINGER : :
   a. shoe : toe
   b. helmet : head
   c. belt : body
   d. cape : shoulders
   e. spectacles : nose

2. BIOGRAPHY : PERSON : :
   a. adventure : heroine
   b. essay : paragraph
   c. history : nation
   d. tragedy : actor
   e. hymn : religion

3. KEYBOARD : OCTAVE : :
   a. violin : string
   b. racetrack : furlong
   c. house : room
   d. wall : brick
   e. bolt : watt

4. FLIP : HURL : :
   a. press : push
   b. sing : chant
   c. nap : snooze
   d. jump : bound
   e. dance : waltz

5. BUSHEL : WHEAT : :
   a. carat : diamond
   b. land : crop
   c. soil : grain
   d. bill : dollar
   e. quantity : harvest

6. WRITING : PAPER : :
   a. flotilla : water
   b. phalanx : grass
   c. inscription : book
   d. design : tile
   e. painting : canvas

7. LIE : FIB : :
   a. rout : defeat
   b. fiasco : enterprise
   c. battle : campaign
   d. apex : nadir
   e. proclamation : declaration

8. PANEL : JURORS : :
   a. caravan : camels
   b. platoon : soldiers
   c. clique : pariahs
   d. entourage : tyros
   e. school : classes

9. FUNNY : HILARIOUS : :
   a. flash : lightning
   b. pony : horse
   c. perfidious : loyal
   d. tentative : temporary
   e. disconcerting : alarming

10. KING : MONARCHY : :
    a. tyrant : dictatorship
    b. president : legislature
    c. pope : papacy
    d. captain : military
    e. teacher : school

11. LISTLESS : FATIGUED : :
    a. weary : sluggish
    b. executive : employee
    c. belligerent : warlike
    d. neurotic : psychotic
    e. vigorous : vivacious

12. ENOBLE : MORTIFY : :
    a. subjugate : conquer
    b. glimmer : radiate
    c. obdurate : reject
    d. redeem : repay
    e. exalt : humiliate

13. SLANG : SPEECH : :
    a. idiom : discourse
    b. accent : voice
    c. argot : vocabulary
    d. wit : humor
    e. clarity : enunciation

14. DOCILE : AGGRESSIVE : :
    a. myopic : observant
    b. strident : harsh
    c. fallow : productive
    d. skeptical : doubtful
    e. meek : rambunctious

15. ENTOURAGE : FOLLOWERS : :
    a. accolade : praises
    b. clique : members
    c. cascade : ripples
    d. cluster : classics
    e. campus : buildings

16. THESAURUS : WORDS : :
    a. novel : characters
    b. handbook : pictures
    c. catalogue : dates
    d. atlas : maps
    e. pamphlet : illustrations

17. JESTER : JOCOSE : :
    a. stoic : capricious
    b. buffoon : intelligent
    c. raconteur : laconic
    d. clown : colorful
    e. zany : ludicrous

18. GARBAGE : MALODOROUS : :
    a. refuse : superfluous
    b. perfume : fragrant
    c. incense : olfactory
    d. waste : useless
    e. fog : moist

19. CRANKY : CANTANKEROUS : :
    a. irascible : peevish
    b. hapless : lucky
    c. infant : sibling
    d. churlish : urbane
    e. impeccable : faultless

20. SIMULATED : SYNTHETIC : :
    a. authentic : imitation
    b. bogus : artificial
    c. leather : plastic
    d. homogeneous : similar
    e. impetuous : reserved

UNIT G

Directions: Select the pair of words that most nearly expresses the relationship of the pair of key words in capital letters. Circle the letter preceding the pair you choose.

1. SONG : ALBUM : :
   a. finger : hand
   b. pencil : case
   c. poem : anthology
   d. opera : orchestra
   e. book : shelf

2. SWAGGER : PRIDE : :
   a. wail : joy
   b. simper : fear
   c. waltz : grace
   d. saunter : diffidence
   e. stammer : sound

3. GALE : WIND : :
   a. trickle : leak
   b. generator : current
   c. tide : wave
   d. branch : twig
   e. blast : gust

4. PODIUM : CONDUCTOR : :
   a. platform : politician
   b. stage : actress
   c. staircase : resident
   d. bench : plaintiff
   e. pedestal : pedestrian

5. QUARANTINE : PATIENT : :
   a. raffle : prize
   b. sequester : jury
   c. rally : cause
   d. parole : prisoner
   e. rebuke : request

6. DEFEAT : DISHEARTENED : :
   a. debate : enlightened
   b. fiasco : overjoyed
   c. victory : elated
   d. battle : triumphant
   e. problem : puzzled

7. PRAISE : EXALT : :
   a. abhor : hate
   b. crawl : walk
   c. admire : worship
   d. study : learn
   e. flood : innundate

8. CURATOR : MUSEUM : :
   a. pilot : plane
   b. principal : school
   c. coach : sport
   d. keeper : zoo
   e. guard : prison

9. HOLSTER : GUN : :
   a. scabbard : sword
   b. cannon : shell
   c. fork : knife
   d. shoe : leather
   e. bow : arrow

10. CULPRIT : STEAL : :
    a. brigand : boast
    b. detective : arrest
    c. sheriff : incarcerate
    d. felon : flee
    e. shoplifter : filch

11. RELIGIOUS : DEVOUT : :
    a. banal : sad
    b. loyal : staunch
    c. convivial : convincing
    d. shriveled : tall
    e. audacious : noisy

12. BOTHER : PLAGUE : :
    a. eulogize : praise
    b. abrogate : abridge
    c. document : prove
    d. interest : fascinate
    e. exalt : cheer

13. OBSESSION : WISH : :
    a. ambition : hedonism
    b. silence : pacificism
    c. hold : embrace
    d. sponsor : endorse
    e. chauvinism : patriotism

14. ANACHRONISM : HISTORY : :
    a. balk : refusal
    b. error : calculation
    c. lapse : judgment
    d. triumph : battle
    e. default : failure

15. MOGUL : TYCOON : :
    a. aristocrat : millionaire
    b. totalitarian : democrat
    c. pariah : outcast
    d. ally : adversary
    e. autocrat : senator

16. SYCHOPHANT : FLATTER : :
    a. recalcitrant : resist
    b. fanatic : revoke
    c. adversary : adhere
    d. catalyst : terminate
    e. debtor : remit

17. UPBRAID : WRONGDOER : :
    a. astound : audience
    b. exalt : paragon
    c. emulate : plan
    d. denounce : pragmatist
    e. remunerate : employee

18. RELIGION : THEOLOGY : :
    a. bird : pathology
    b. microscope : biology
    c. disease : ethnology
    d. plant : geology
    e. word : etymology

19. SYNOD : CONVENTION : :
    a. convocation : ceremony
    b. dispersing : gathering
    c. house : room
    d. priest : minister
    e. clergy : layperson

20. OPULENT : SQUALID : :
    a. puzzling : enigmatic
    b. obsolete : archaic
    c. similar : congruous
    d. garish : austere
    e. amorous : amorphous

UNIT H

Directions: Select the pair of words that most nearly expresses the relationship of the pair of key words in capital letters. Circle the letter preceding the pair you choose.

1. DRY : PARCHED : :
   a. devoid : worthless
   b. cold : frozen
   c. bare : sparse
   d. mediocre : ordinary
   e. martial : warlike

2. DOG : KENNEL : :
   a. lion : zoo
   b. bird : aviary
   c. bee : flower
   d. water : tank
   e. shark : ocean

3. STREAM : RIVER : :
   a. puddle : sink
   b. pond : puddle
   c. wave : current
   d. lake : ocean
   e. rill : brook

4. JOURNEY : MAP : :
   a. assault : army
   b. army : manual
   c. dates : almanac
   d. information : directory
   e. meal : cookbook

5. EXPERIMENT : LABORATORY : :
   a. recovery : hospital
   b. exercise : gymnasium
   c. chance : casino
   d. relaxation : hotel
   e. attendance : school

6. TORRID : WARM : :
   a. cold : frigid
   b. snow : ice
   c. hot : tepid
   d. moist : damp
   e. brick : stone

7. MENACE : ENEMY : :
   a. ally : friend
   b. pioneer : explorer
   c. bachelor : spouse
   d. journalist : writer
   e. volunteer : patriot

8. CONCRETE : RIGID : :
   a. water : blue
   b. wood : oak
   c. clay : plastic
   d. cotton : cloth
   e. wood : brittle

9. FELONY : THIEF : :
   a. knowledge : scholar
   b. worry : optimist
   c. injury : sadist
   d. belief : agnostic
   e. illness : germ

10. AMAZON : BUXOM : :
    a. gymnast : rotund
    b. ballerina : svelte
    c. wrestler : cadaverous
    d. psychic : articulate
    e. teller : inefficient

11. LEARNING : CLASSROOM : :
    a. exercise : stadium
    b. medicine : hospital
    c. books : library
    d. convention : hotel
    e. litigation : courtroom

12. SORROW : MERRIMENT : :
    a. suppression : rejection
    b. depression : elation
    c. subjugation : freedom
    d. abstinence : withdrawal
    e. affluence : poverty

13. LIQUID : SQUIRT : :
    a. ocean : tide
    b. ripple : wave
    c. deluge : torrent
    d. debacle : disaster
    e. blood : spate

14. GYRATE : WHIRL : :
    a. meditate : decide
    b. consecrate : arrange
    c. peregrinate : walk
    d. procrastinate : extend
    e. collate : order

15. MAGNATE : CORPORATION : :
    a. infidel : federation
    b. celibate : prison
    c. manager : company
    d. potentate : kingdom
    e. tyro : orchestra

16. PAUPER : INDIGENCE : :
    a. zealot : apathy
    b. sluggard : lassitude
    c. tycoon : industry
    d. chef : cuisine
    e. gambler : cards

17. TRAVEL : MEANDER : :
    a. study : memorize
    b. survey : observe
    c. speak : digress
    d. alphabetize : arrange
    e. destroy : shatter

18. PROGENY : CHILDREN : :
    a. clique : adversaries
    b. entourage : heroes
    c. concert : artists
    d. posterity : parents
    e. coterie : followers

19. DOLT : OBTUSE : :
    a. buffoon : active
    b. wizard : acute
    c. brigand : veracious
    d. pedant : juvenile
    e. oaf : urbane

20. PREVARICATOR : INTEGRITY : :
    a. veteran : experience
    b. champion : challenger
    c. artisan : skill
    d. charlatan : honesty
    e. sage : wisdom

UNIT I

Directions: Select the pair of words that most nearly expresses the relationship of the pair of key words in capital letters. Circle the letter preceding the pair you choose.

1. POLITICS : GRAFT : :
   a. competition : trophy
   b. battle : wounds
   c. war : booty
   d. explosion : fallout
   e. valor : recognition

2. DISMOUNT : HORSE : :
   a. disembark : ship
   b. desert : army
   c. escape : jail
   d. descend : staircase
   e. matriculate : college

3. LIBRARIAN : BOOKS : :
   a. lawyer : clients
   b. doctor : patients
   c. teacher : students
   d. accountant : figures
   e. pilot : passengers

4. STETHOSCOPE : DOCTOR : :
   a. pestle : pharmacist
   b. jurisprudence : attorney
   c. laboratory : biologist
   d. account : cashier
   e. knowledge : librarian

5. FISH : MERMAID : :
   a. dog : wolf
   b. horse : zebra
   c. ghost : goblin
   d. hero : Superman
   e. horse : centaur

6. ALPHABET : LETTERS : :
   a. list : names
   b. scale : notes
   c. column : numbers
   d. den : thieves
   e. sequence : tenses

7. CONSTRUE : INTERPRET : :
   a. dissect : construct
   b. elucidate : confuse
   c. explicate : analyze
   d. discern : reject
   e. allude : deceive

8. PENITENT : CONTRITE : :
   a. transgressor : amiable
   b. mourner : disconsolate
   c. despot : powerful
   d. egotist : altruistic
   e. hypocrite : outspoken

9. BASEBALL GAME : INNING : :
   a. series : episode
   b. pie : slice
   c. piece : puzzle
   d. class : pupil
   e. sentence : word

10. RECONDITE : SIMPLE : :
    a. cheerful : joyous
    b. abstruse : obvious
    c. florid : ruddy
    d. engrossing : interesting
    e. congenial : companionable

11. BUFFOON : SERIOUS : :
    a. fanatic : moderate
    b. constituent : loyal
    c. panel : smooth
    d. fox : ferocious
    e. tragedian : frivolous

12. REVISION : NOVEL : :
    a. solution : puzzle
    b. formulation : policy
    c. construction : road
    d. alteration : suit
    e. rejection : request

13. BURLY : HUSKY : :
    a. bumptious : foolish
    b. avid : uninterested
    c. corpulent : jolly
    d. cherubic : youthful
    e. lank : lean

14. GOWN : DIAPHONOUS : :
    a. coat : protective
    b. blouse : mottled
    c. veil : gossamer
    d. sombrero : shady
    e. cape : formal

15. EXEMPTION : TAX : :
    a. resistance : authority
    b. compliance : law
    c. adaptation : environment
    d. question : answer
    e. immunity : disease

16. GULLIBLE : NOVICE : :
    a. ingenious : connoisseur
    b. valiant : warrior
    c. experienced : tyro
    d. sanitary : nurse
    e. knowledgeable : veteran

17. SAMARITAN : KIND : :
    a. mute : vehement
    b. altruist : selfish
    c. philanthropist : munificent
    d. teamster : truculent
    e. matriarch : ravenous

18. HOMONYN : SOUND : :
    a. antonym : words
    b. synonym : meaning
    c. acronym : letters
    d. pseudonym : name
    e. metaphor : image

19. CRASS : BOOR : :
    a. coarse : oaf
    b. sophisticated : patriarch
    c. convivial : felon
    d. inexperienced : infant
    e. fearless : brigand

20. ANGER : PIQUE : :
    a. deference : praise
    b. ecstasy : joy
    c. amusement : acceptance
    d. evil : heinous
    e. insidious : treacherous

UNIT J

Directions: Select the pair of words that most nearly expresses the relationship of the pair of key words in capital letters. Circle the letter preceding the pair you choose.

1. HIGHWAY : ROAD : :
   a. hole : pit
   b. escalator : elevator
   c. banquet : meal
   d. kettle : cauldron
   e. lane : path

2. POND : LAKE : :
   a. shoe : boot
   b. sea : ocean
   c. rock : boulder
   d. field : meadow
   e. sofa : chair

3. SUITCASE : TRUNK : :
   a. purse : pocket
   b. vault : safe
   c. bag : sack
   d. bib : towel
   e. finger : thumb

4. WATER : DROWN : :
   a. fire : immolate
   b. air : breathe
   c. earth : travel
   d. grass : mow
   e. stone : shatter

5. STAMMER : TALK : :
   a. tramp : dance
   b. dream : sleep
   c. limp : walk
   d. miscalculate : err
   e. swallow : swim

6. AIRPLANE : HANGAR : :
   a. water : canteen
   b. dinghy : dock
   c. wrench : garage
   d. sail : mast
   e. salt : shaker

7. ALIBI : EXCUSE : :
   a. pillar : strength
   b. tirade : explanation
   c. enigma : puzzle
   d. dilemma : solution
   e. conundrum : explanation

8. DESTITUTE : VAGRANT : :
   a. prosperous : squatter
   b. congenial : tenant
   c. affluent : tourist
   d. outdoors : camper
   e. maritime : sailor

9. OBSCURE : MANIFEST : :
   a. slanted : awry
   b. ancient : nebulous
   c. amazed : agog
   d. ambiguous : adverse
   e. symmetrical : askew

10. ROB : RAVISH : :
    a. defer : oppose
    b. dissent : disagree
    c. singe : burn
    d. chatter : banter
    e. demolish : raze

11. NONENTITY : CELEBRITY : :
    a. president : queen
    b. alternate : substitute
    c. criminal : embezzler
    d. extra : star
    e. star : galaxy

12. INGRATE : THANKLESS : :
    a. martinet : obliging
    b. hoyden : boisterous
    c. abbot : secular
    d. despot : deranged
    e. warden : official

13. INGENUOUS : NAIVE : :
    a. fervent : averse
    b. apathetic : sad
    c. candid : frank
    d. compassionate : social
    e. contrite : determined

14. SIREN : ATTRACTIVE : :
    a. ingenue : aged
    b. pedant : childish
    c. hag : charming
    d. titan : powerful
    e. hag : ugly

15. PITHY : MAXIM : :
    a. frivolous : epitaph
    b. meaningful : proverb
    c. historical : saga
    d. dramatic : oration
    e. ancient : epic

16. GREGARIOUS : FRIENDS : :
    a. mysterious : strangers
    b. fractious : enemies
    c. diligent : partisans
    d. valiant : allies
    e. archaic : artisans

17. MENDICANT : BEG : :
    a. marauder : plunder
    b. urchin : swim
    c. corsair : run
    d. valet : scurry
    e. nomad : meditate

18. CRONE : WIZENED : :
    a. dotard : perspicacious
    b. octogenarian : shriveled
    c. ingenue : masculine
    d. chauvinist : cheerful
    e. imbiber : wet

19. GLUTTONOUS : ROTUND : :
    a. diffident : lonely
    b. amorphous : deadly
    c. abstemious : lank
    d. lugubrious : sad
    e. cantankerous : cheerful

20. FISCAL : MONEY : :
    a. geological : solar system
    b. practical : practice
    c. gustatory : atmosphere
    d. astronomical : aviation
    e. conjugal : marriage

UNIT K

Directions: Select the pair of words that most nearly expresses the relationship of the pair of key words in capital letters. Circle the letter preceding the pair you choose.

1. HOSPITAL : DOCTOR : :
   a. library : reader
   b. courthouse : judge
   c. stadium : fan
   d. market : vendor
   e. church : atheist

2. STRIPED : ZEBRA : :
   a. industrious : beaver
   b. spotted : leopard
   c. courageous : lion
   d. weighty : elephant
   e. fragmented : glass

3. ACT : PLAY : :
   a. fact : diary
   b. date : volume
   c. chapter : book
   d. poem : verse
   e. car : train

4. MUSTARD : CONDIMENT : :
   a. clove : spice
   b. acorn : oak
   c. nut : shell
   d. ice cream : treat
   e. soda : liquid

5. UNITED STATES : DOLLAR : :
   a. Mexico : peso
   b. Japan : shilling
   c. France : pound
   d. Germany : coin
   e. England : money

6. TOSS : HURL : :
   a. augment : add
   b. punch : tap
   c. moon : sun
   d. moan : sigh
   e. question : grill

7. CONVICT : JAIL : :
   a. executive : atrium
   b. neurotic : office
   c. athlete : gymnasium
   d. tombstone : cemetery
   e. psychotic : asylum

8. FILTH : SQUALID : :
   a. light : bright
   b. moisture : dampness
   c. cleanliness : antiseptic
   d. hovel : cottage
   e. garbage : trash

9. CREDIT : DEBIT : :
   a. stock : bond
   b. intermission : hiatus
   c. broker : client
   d. finance : money
   e. augment : decrease

10. HIGHWAY : HORIZONTAL : :
    a. skyscraper : vertical
    b. cave : mysterious
    c. bridge : suspended
    d. cathedral : Gothic
    e. mansion : luxurious

11. TRAITOR : BETRAYS : :
    a. bandage : adheres
    b. coward : defies
    c. legacy : enriches
    d. aristocrat : governs
    e. renegade : deserts

12. CONDUCTOR : BATON : :
    a. referee : whistle
    b. farmer : rake
    c. rower : oar
    d. mechanic : wrench
    e. monarch : scepter

13. REMARK : SCURRILOUS : :
    a. appetite : voracious
    b. illness : congenital
    c. statement : solemn
    d. comment : caustic
    e. proclamation : hilarious

14. RUNNER : FLEET : :
    a. artist : talented
    b. ballerina : slim
    c. acrobat : supple
    d. caretaker : efficient
    e. sheriff : brave

15. CITADEL : FORTRESS : :
    a. wall : prison
    b. bastion : hillside
    c. basement : foundation
    d. mortar : wall
    e. vault : dungeon

16. INVALID : HEALTH : :
    a. martinet : severity
    b. pariah : friendship
    c. hero : fortitude
    d. democracy : equality
    e. adversary : hatred

17. ADAGE : SIGNIFICANT : :
    a. essay : archaic
    b. platitude : trite
    c. maxim : meaningful
    d. sermon : inspirational
    e. epitaph : poetic

18. EMBRACE : SWEETHEART : :
    a. assault : adversary
    b. admire : protagonist
    c. worship : clergyperson
    d. emulate : champion
    e. fondle : philatelist

19. FOOL : OBTUSE : :
    a. moron : perceptive
    b. sage : acute
    c. scholar : charismatic
    d. boor : urbane
    e. student : assiduous

20. ODOR : FETID : :
    a. patient : chronic
    b. aroma : haughty
    c. feeling : remorseful
    d. wind : tempestuous
    e. smell : noisome

UNIT L

Directions: Select the pair of words that most nearly expresses the relationship of the pair of key words in capital letters. Circle the letter preceding the pair you choose.

1. TREE : FOREST : :
   a. individual : crowd
   b. classroom : school
   c. chorus : duet
   d. leader : mob
   e. pastor : congregation

2. TRIAL : JUDGE : :
   a. debate : partisan
   b. eulogy : speaker
   c. congress : senator
   d. ring : pugilist
   e. contest : referee

3. WATER : PIPE : :
   a. train : rails
   b. electricity : wires
   c. waste : sewer
   d. pearl : necklace
   e. blood : artery

4. CONCERT : MUSIC : :
   a. symphony : musicians
   b. exhibition : painting
   c. bazaar : merchants
   d. gallery : patrons
   e. banquet : diners

5. PROLOGUE : PLAY : :
   a. justice : law
   b. preamble : constitution
   c. aria : opera
   d. debate : legislation
   e. journey : arrival

6. MINE : SALT : :
   a. kiln : brick
   b. soil : sand
   c. quarry : marble
   d. ocean : fish
   e. ore : iron

7. WEATHERVANE : ROOF : :
   a. thermometer : wall
   b. crescent : sky
   c. star : universe
   d. crypt : cellar
   e. cross : steeple

8. EXPLICIT : INDEFINITE : :
   a. specific : exact
   b. weak : fragile
   c. wise : intelligent
   d. feeble : strong
   e. coherent : clear

9. THRIFTY : NIGGARDLY : :
   a. worthless : priceless
   b. expensive : exorbitant
   c. outstanding : excellent
   d. precious : valuable
   e. thoughtful : pensive

10. POIGNANT : DRAMA : :
    a. blasphemous : comedy
    b. soporific : ballet
    c. maudlin : tragedy
    d. musical : symphony
    e. musical : review

11. INCARCERATE : CELL : :
    a. bury : treasure
    b. inter : tomb
    c. store : shelf
    d. preserve : jar
    e. save : bank

12. NEFARIOUS : CRIMINAL : :
    a. discreet : disciple
    b. legal : legislator
    c. admirable : paragon
    d. penurious : tycoon
    e. imaginary : mirage

13. SQUALID : HOVEL : :
    a. ancient : castle
    b. opulent : mansion
    c. penitent : prison
    d. oval : stadium
    e. portable : tent

14. FORMER : ERSTWHILE : :
    a. previous : subsequent
    b. future : prediction
    c. glib : nonchalant
    d. nostalgic : wistful
    e. lucid : nebulous

15. BONBON : CANDY BAR : :
    a. drama : play
    b. dwarf : elf
    c. wheel : tire
    d. vignette : novel
    e. rubber : chewing gum

16. HERO : INTREPID : :
    a. murderer : infamous
    b. soldier : marital
    c. detective : inspector
    d. felon : feckless
    e. drunkard : sober

17. IMPEACH : TRY : :
    a. convict : jail
    b. arraign : charge
    c. defer : reject
    d. consider : decide
    e. legislate : debate

18. EXUBERANT : DISGRUNTLED : :
    a. macabre : gory
    b. latent : modern
    c. itinerant : magnanimous
    d. succinct : verbose
    e. effusive : taciturn

19. BOWDLERIZE : BOOK : :
    a. abridge : novel
    b. patronize : theatre
    c. stigmatize : celebrity
    d. withdraw : publication
    e. expurgate : film

20. OBSEQUIOUS : SERVANT : :
    a. cooperative : colleague
    b. omnipotent : monarch
    c. mordant : worker
    d. valorous : dastard
    e. servile : employee

UNIT M

Directions: Select the pair of words that most nearly expresses the relationship of the pair of key words in capital letters. Circle the letter preceding the pair you choose.

1. COIN : METAL : :
   a. quilt : cloth
   b. penny : monetary
   c. dollar : currency
   d. bill : paper
   e. dime : money

2. RAKE : FORK : :
   a. plank : floor
   b. baton : band
   c. cudgel : bat
   d. cameo : stone
   e. chisel : hammer

3. TIME : CLOCK : :
   a. germs : microscope
   b. weather : odometer
   c. temperature : thermometer
   d. days : calendar
   e. stars : telescope

4. MARATHON : SPRINT : :
   a. skip : leap
   b. shriek : whisper
   c. banquet : meal
   d. braid : hair
   e. trek : stroll

5. CHAPEL : CHURCH : :
   a. palace : villa
   b. cottage : mansion
   c. chimes : bells
   d. canoe : dinghy
   e. elf : giant

6. ADJUDGE : CONSIDER : :
   a. plan : outline
   b. sentence : acquit
   c. decide : plan
   d. conclude : discuss
   e. reject : debate

7. PROGNOSIS : DISEASE : :
   a. forecast : event
   b. cause : effect
   c. sedative : sleep
   d. statement : fact
   e. horoscope : event

8. REPUGNANCE : AVERSION : :
   a. zeal : ardor
   b. scholar : teacher
   c. loyalty : capriciousness
   d. hilarity : urbanity
   e. esteem : disdain

9. SOBRIQUET : PERSON : :
   a. epithet : description
   b. signature : name
   c. alias : criminal
   d. trademark : product
   e. surname : family name

10. SALESPERSON : COMMISSION : :
    a. celebrity : fame
    b. novelist : readers
    c. teller : funds
    d. rabbi : alms
    e. author : royalty

11. APERTURE : CAMERA : :
    a. book : list
    b. cavity : tooth
    c. typewriter : keyboard
    d. rudder : ship
    e. window : house

12. DEBUTANTE : DOWAGER : :
    a. girl : lass
    b. youth : age
    c. male : female
    d. infancy : childhood
    e. facts : knowledge

13. HYPOTHESIS : TRUTH : :
    a. accusation : charge
    b. allegation : truth
    c. assault : victory
    d. attack : defeat
    e. thought : idea

14. APIARY : BEES : :
    a. zoo : lions
    b. aviary : birds
    c. web : spider
    d. mound : insects
    e. fiduciary : fish

15. VIRTUOSO : INEPT : :
    a. dilettante : serious
    b. pedant : liberal
    c. skeptic : cynical
    d. bulb : incandescent
    e. entrepreneur : independent

16. INVITATION : HOSTESS : :
    a. devotion : relative
    b. acceptance : guest
    c. trespass : neighbor
    d. compliance : friend
    e. obedience : robot

17. MAGNANIMOUS : BENEFACTOR : :
    a. powerful : malefactor
    b. mutable : instigator
    c. helpful : mendicant
    d. reclusive : hermit
    e. spritely : pedestrian

18. TAUTOLOGY : CONCISE : :
    a. verbosity : succinct
    b. posture : poor
    c. exposition : flamboyant
    d. lucidity : clarity
    e. arctic : frigid

19. DESTRUCTIVE : SUBVERSIVE : :
    a. inductive : logical
    b. rapacious : subdued
    c. mendacious : deceitful
    d. assertive : passive
    e. ironic : dominant

20. MENDICANT : BEG : :
    a. crony : correct
    b. neophyte : rebel
    c. prodigal : conserve
    d. sycophant : flatter
    e. potentate : attack

UNIT N

Directions: Select the pair of words that most nearly expresses the relationship of the pair of key words in capital letters. Circle the letter preceding the pair you choose.

1. DRAWL : SPEECH : :
   a. tilt : jolt
   b. slink : walk
   c. wave : shake
   d. reject : defy
   e. drizzle : rain

2. BREAD : MOLD : :
   a. jail : bars
   b. apple : shine
   c. grass : dew
   d. muscle : strength
   e. iron : rust

3. PITCH : ROOF : :
   a. drop : cliff
   b. level : floor
   c. torso : heap
   d. summit : mountain
   e. grade : highway

4. ANGER : RAGE : :
   a. pleasure : ecstasy
   b. fear : potency
   c. shame : defeat
   d. cuisine : menu
   e. stress : nerve

5. SCIENTIST : FACTS : :
   a. sheriff : criminals
   b. detective : clues
   c. orthodontist : teeth
   d. accountant : details
   e. cook : utensils

6. DESPISE : CHERISH : :
   a. magnify : observe
   b. extemporize : convince
   c. intrude : evaluate
   d. uphold : maintain
   e. revive : extinguish

7. DRIZZLE : CLOUDBURST : :
   a. imp : giant
   b. defeat : disaster
   c. hut : house
   d. hurricane : wind
   e. mist : fog

8. ALTITUDE : MOUNTAIN : :
   a. molecules : water
   b. solution : equation
   c. depth : ocean
   d. mud : marsh
   e. current : brook

9. CURRENT : OBSOLETE : :
   a. motor : sail
   b. contemporary : historical
   c. traditional : ancient
   d. archaic : outmoded
   e. modern : timely

10. VOLCANO : LAVA : :
    a. explosion : destruction
    b. cobra : poison
    c. radio : sound
    d. bottle : wine
    e. geyser : water

11. CONVERSATION : DISCOURSE : :
    a. secret : silence
    b. gossip : scandal
    c. song : music
    d. jabber : gibberish
    e. patter : debate

12. WAVE : CREST : :
    a. mountain : peak
    b. pond : surface
    c. rose : thorn
    d. head : hair
    e. valley : summit

13. HEEL : ACHILLES : :
    a. humor : Twain
    b. hair : Samson
    c. mystery : Poe
    d. honesty : Washington
    e. love : Romeo

14. COTERIE : COMPANIONS : :
    a. pack : sheep
    b. sorority : students
    c. retinue : enemies
    d. university : classes
    e. herd : cattle

15. PLACID : SERENE : :
    a. illusory : unreal
    b. lake : ocean
    c. turbulent : calm
    d. peaceful : tranquil
    e. hybrid : mixed

16. CRUCIAL : MOMENTOUS : :
    a. coersive : forceful
    b. calculated : flattering
    c. trivial : important
    d. significant : vital
    e. fan : celebrity

17. VILLAIN : INIQUITOUS : :
    a. hag : pitiful
    b. vixen : victorious
    c. felon : felicitous
    d. demon : celestial
    e. miser : niggardly

18. INSULT : REVILE : :
    a. eulogize : approve
    b. castigate : praise
    c. chide : scold
    d. censure : restrict
    e. admonish : envy

19. LAMPOON : SATIRE : :
    a. prelude : introduction
    b. eulogy : speech
    c. gibe : joke
    d. sonnet : poem
    e. dirge : lament

20. MISANTHROPE : HUMANKIND : :
    a. philatelist : stamps
    b. misogynist : women
    c. numismatist : numbers
    d. curator : exhibits
    e. prospector : gold

UNIT O

Directions: Select the pair of words that most nearly expresses the relationship of the pair of key words in capital letters. Circle the letter preceding the pair you choose.

1. SUMMIT : MOUNTAIN : :
   a. window : wall
   b. salon : mansion
   c. vault : cellar
   d. roof : house
   e. patio : villa

2. ARSENAL : ARMS : :
   a. bazaar : bargains
   b. library : books
   c. stadium : sports
   d. cabinet : medicines
   e. market : patrons

3. SKIT : PLAY : :
   a. smock : cape
   b. dancer : troupe
   c. opera : aria
   d. singer : chorus
   e. tale : novel

4. TOWN : CITY : :
   a. hamlet : village
   b. pamphlet : almanac
   c. residence : community
   d. growth : tumor
   e. quiz : test

5. WHISPER : RANT : :
   a. clang : tinkle
   b. weep : cry
   c. mumble : shout
   d. sing : chant
   e. contemplate : think

6. GUARD : PRISON : :
   a. monitor : post
   b. sentry : camp
   c. criminologist : crime
   d. vault : treasure
   e. jockey : horse

7. FAREWELL : GREETINGS : :
   a. commencement : termination
   b. prelude : preface
   c. arrival : departure
   d. preamble : index
   e. conclusion : introduction

8. CLICHE´ : BANAL : :
   a. fable : ancient
   b. drama : concise
   c. telegram : significant
   d. epigram : witty
   e. soliloquy : loud

9. PRELUDE : AFTERMATH : :
   a. glossary : data
   b. overture : epilogue
   c. appendix : afterword
   d. intermission : drama
   e. preface : introduction

10. GHOSTLY : SPECTRAL : :
    a. tranquil : widespread
    b. renowned : superior
    c. remunerative : plural
    d. translucent : opaque
    e. transparent : diaphonous

11. COQUETTE : FLIRTATIOUS : :
    a. youth : callow
    b. maiden : immature
    c. siren : strident
    d. nun : devoted
    e. matron : orderly

12. TALLY : RESULTS : :
    a. predict : events
    b. tabulate : figures
    c. hoard : possessions
    d. analyze : motives
    e. accumulate : facts

13. TITAN : DWARF : :
    a. vessel : ship
    b. elephant : mouse
    c. romance : love
    d. dragon : myth
    e. energetic : lethargic

14. ADMIRE : ADULATE : :
    a. gyrate : whirl
    b. radiate : glow
    c. celebrate : lionize
    d. hesitate : pause
    e. substitute : remove

15. PARCHMENT : PAPER : :
    a. pencil : crayon
    b. quill : pen
    c. write : inscribe
    d. crossbow : gun
    e. astrology : astronomy

16. AVERSION : LIKING : :
    a. rejection : elation
    b. preference : choice
    c. predilection : distaste
    d. election : antagonistic
    e. lassitude : lethargy

17. CRIMINOLOGIST : FELONS : :
    a. bacteriologist : germs
    b. philologist : birds
    c. anthropologist : fish
    d. etymologist : insects
    e. sociologist : theories

18. CENSOR : EXPURGATE : :
    a. adapt : accept
    b. expand : continue
    c. abridge : condense
    d. revise : improve
    e. renovate : modernize

19. MASTODON : ELF : :
    a. hut : cottage
    b. carpet : rug
    c. hound : dog
    d. year : month
    e. behemoth : midget

20. CACOPHONY : NOISE : :
    a. euphony : music
    b. dust : dirt
    c. aroma : air
    d. harmony : tempo
    e. darkness : shade

UNIT P

Directions: Select the pair of words that most nearly expresses the relationship of the pair of key words in capital letters. Circle the letter preceding the pair you choose.

1. BUOY : HARBOR : :
   a. carpet : aisle
   b. sign : wall
   c. billboard : highway
   d. detour : road
   e. pebble : shoe

2. MYTH : HISTORY : :
   a. anecdote : essay
   b. tangible : real
   c. nonfiction : reality
   d. Lincoln : Cupid
   e. fancy : fact

3. CAFFEINE : COFFEE : :
   a. nicotine : tobacco
   b. gold : earth
   c. air : vacuum
   d. tobacco : cigar
   e. alcohol : drunkard

4. GUITAR : STRINGS : :
   a. trumpet : volume
   b. piano : keys
   c. briefcase : handles
   d. catalog : volumes
   e. violin : tone

5. PROLOGUE : DRAMA : :
   a. preamble : constitution
   b. menu : dinner
   c. handshake : conversation
   d. door : house
   e. paragraph : story

6. DIVORCE : MARRIAGE : :
   a. merger : company
   b. estrangement : friendship
   c. loathing : hatred
   d. bankruptcy : partnership
   e. child : family

7. AUDITORIUM : BALCONY : :
   a. valley : mountain
   b. lobby : auditorium
   c. cellar : roof
   d. wall : ceiling
   e. orchestra : mezzanine

8. REFLECTION : LIGHT : :
   a. echo : sound
   b. wave : water
   c. volume : noise
   d. splinter : wound
   e. image : mirror

9. SLUR : ENUNCIATE : :
   a. speak : sing
   b. whisper : talk
   c. sprawl : sit
   d. groan : sigh
   e. stumble : walk

10. MEMO : LETTER : :
    a. math : calculus
    b. pamphlet : tome
    c. note : card
    d. cup : goblet
    e. epitaph : inscription

11. LIGHT : INCANDESCENT : :
    a. sun : radiant
    b. water : current
    c. gloom : constant
    d. ice : glacial
    e. digestion : health

12. JOIN : MOVEMENT : :
    a. articulate : friendship
    b. dissent : majority
    c. espouse : cause
    d. cooperate : teammate
    e. support : candidate

13. ACCEDE : REQUEST : :
    a. surrender : army
    b. undertake : enterprise
    c. consider : plea
    d. deny : obligation
    e. grant : petition

14. SHOPLIFTER : FURTIVE : :
    a. client : gullible
    b. manager : authoritative
    c. shopper : fastidious
    d. customer : overt
    e. salesperson : persuasive

15. POETRY : STANZA : :
    a. debut : society
    b. employee : company
    c. prose : paragraph
    d. opera : song
    e. edition : book

16. BLITHE : SAD : :
    a. horrible : ugly
    b. slovenly : neat
    c. tedious : dull
    d. gigantic : microscopic
    e. flippant : austere

17. METICULOUS : PAINSTAKING : :
    a. omniverous : thoughtful
    b. diffident : courageous
    c. slovenly : careless
    d. morbid : cheerful
    e. carniverous : hungry

18. CHIVALROUS : GALLANT : :
    a. insolent : considerate
    b. courteous : gracious
    c. animate : lively
    d. dogmatic : reasonable
    e. knight : lord

19. SALUBRIOUS : DELETERIOUS : :
    a. indigenous : native
    b. pious : religious
    c. jaded : worn
    d. volatile : explosive
    e. cryptic : understandable

20. EVASIVE : TRUTHFUL : :
    a. glib : articulate
    b. pensive : thoughtful
    c. reticent : loquacious
    d. diligent : assiduous
    e. perfunctory : superficial

UNIT Q

Directions: Select the pair of words that most nearly expresses the relationship of the pair of key words in capital letters. Circle the letter preceding the pair you choose.

1. HUB : WHEEL : :
   a. orbit : planet
   b. spine : person
   c. axis : earth
   d. pole : tent
   e. rafter : roof

2. SAND : POWDER : :
   a. pages : book
   b. sawdust : flour
   c. drops : rain
   d. beads : necklace
   e. pebble : rock

3. PIRATE : SAILOR : :
   a. doctor : surgeon
   b. weed : plant
   c. bush : tree
   d. damp : dry
   e. winter : spring

4. EXILE : SANCTUARY : :
   a. refugee : haven
   b. traveler : itinerary
   c. convict : cell
   d. stowaway : cabin
   e. tramp : road

5. MIME : PERFORMER : :
   a. knight : plebian
   b. ballerina : athlete
   c. manager : subordinate
   d. dietician : advisor
   e. potter : artisan

6. PRESIDENT : INAUGURATION : :
   a. priest : ordination
   b. freshman : matriculation
   c. student : graduation
   d. candidate : election
   e. bride : matrimony

7. AUTOMOBILE : PARKING SPACE : :
   a. horse : racetrack
   b. chariot : buggy
   c. trophy : shelf
   d. rocket : air
   e. boat : berth

8. BOOK : GLOSSARY : :
   a. nomenclature : name
   b. newspaper : edition
   c. map : legend
   d. globe : degree
   e. lexicon : words

9. DRAFT : NOVEL : :
   a. attempt : success
   b. index : book
   c. grades : transcript
   d. music : opera
   e. rehearsal : play

10. PRAY : CHAPEL : :
    a. relax : beach
    b. dream : siesta
    c. worship : Sunday
    d. drink : glass
    e. dine : café

11. SMOKESTACK : CHIMNEY : :
    a. flame : fire
    b. engine : machinery
    c. boiler : basement
    d. cauldron : kettle
    e. coal : wood

12. HOMICIDE : MURDERER : :
    a. robbery : convict
    b. theft : spy
    c. fraud : liar
    d. atrocity : villain
    e. felony : thief

13. DOOR : THEATRE : :
    a. elevator : store
    b. window : room
    c. turnstile : stadium
    d. escalator : building
    e. staircase : balcony

14. HELMET : HEAD : :
    a. heel : shoe
    b. spur : boot
    c. knife : sheath
    d. epaulet : shoulder
    e. uniform : costume

15. VISITOR : RESIDENT : :
    a. stranger : enemy
    b. guest : host
    c. traveler : voyager
    d. cloud : sky
    e. porter : hotel

16. BATTER : MUD : :
    a. lotion : soap
    b. water : fluid
    c. milk : coffee
    d. wool : cloth
    e. paste : glue

17. RELIGIOUS : SECULAR : :
    a. military : aggressive
    b. eternal : infinite
    c. humorless : austere
    d. celestial : mundane
    e. motley : talkative

18. ORATOR : RHETORICAL : :
    a. teamster : cooperative
    b. expert : maladroit
    c. acrobat : agile
    d. coxswain : corpulent
    e. reporter : accurate

19. ADJOINING : CONTIGUOUS : :
    a. contemptuous : fierce
    b. sluggish : heavy
    c. insipid : damp
    d. adjacent : neighborly
    e. acrimonious : bitter

20. HYPERBOLE : EXAGGERATION : :
    a. curse : epithet
    b. euphemism : understatement
    c. simile : metaphor
    d. warrant : deception
    e. proverb : ancient

UNIT R

Directions: Select the pair of words that most nearly expresses the relationship of the pair of key words in capital letters. Circle the letter preceding the pair you choose.

1. SMOKE : CHIMNEY : :
   a. blood : heart
   b. liquid : siphon
   c. water : ocean
   d. electricity : generator
   e. soup : bowl

2. INVESTOR : BROKER : :
   a. lawyer : litigant
   b. pupil : teacher
   c. citizen : president
   d. private : sargeant
   e. doctor : patient

3. RECEPTIONIST : OFFICE : :
   a. hostess : restaurant
   b. doorperson : entrance
   c. janitor : basement
   d. bartender : bar
   e. porter : terminal

4. TIDE : FLOOD : :
   a. current : ocean
   b. sound : crescendo
   c. drizzle : fog
   d. fire : blaze
   e. wave : ripple

5. DISASTER : LOOM : :
   a. battle : destroy
   b. rupture : sever
   c. fiasco : humiliate
   d. defeat : ensue
   e. catastrophe : impend

6. FRIGID : COOL : :
   a. livid : pale
   b. radiant : bright
   c. horrible : evil
   d. torrid : tepid
   e. inconstant : steady

7. FRESHMAN : SENIOR : :
   a. modern : archaic
   b. recruit : veteran
   c. convert : missionary
   d. twig : branch
   e. basement : attic

8. BUTCHER : CLEAVER : :
   a. hospital : stethoscope
   b. cobbler : awl
   c. surgeon : scalpel
   d. pharmacist : prescription
   e. patient : doctor

9. HELMET : HAT : :
   a. cap : hood
   b. record : disc
   c. medal : chest
   d. muffler : scarf
   e. gauntlet : glove

10. GENTLEMAN : UNCOUTH : :
    a. miser : munificent
    b. chauvinist : patriotic
    c. coward : craven
    d. egotist : selfish
    e. martyr : heroic

11. MEDLEY : SONG : :
    a. anthology : book
    b. portfolio : letter
    c. dozen : eggs
    d. hash : potato
    e. chorus : tenor

12. HOUSE : RAMSHACKLE : :
    a. suit : threadbare
    b. person : elderly
    c. automobile : used
    d. dress : unfashionable
    e. gaslight : obsolete

13. LACONIC : TALKATIVE : :
    a. secure : precarious
    b. commentator : auctioneer
    c. terse : prolix
    d. ruddy : anemic
    e. mobile : stationary

14. BEVY : GROUP : :
    a. class : seminar
    b. audience : mob
    c. army : regiment
    d. college : university
    e. throng : crowd

15. CARELESS : NEGLECTFUL : :
    a. negligent : remiss
    b. moronic : foolish
    c. meticulous : slovenly
    d. infant : adult
    e. impertinent : docile

16. KLEPTOMANIAC : STEAL : :
    a. missionary : preach
    b. brigand : murder
    c. scribe : write
    d. somnambulist : walk
    e. magician : entertain

17. ECSTASY : JOY : :
    a. elation : sadness
    b. affluence : poverty
    c. dejection : gloom
    d. disgruntled : triumph
    e. voluble : volume

18. UNCOUTH : CRASS : :
    a. Lilliputian : verdant
    b. odious : repugnant
    c. laconic : redundant
    d. infamous : envious
    e. malevolent : generous

19. VINDICTIVE : REVENGE : :
    a. forlorn : envy
    b. clement : forgive
    c. reflective : shine
    d. aggressive : run
    e. contemplative : hate

20. REDRESS : REMEDY : :
    a. aggravate : annoy
    b. enhance : charm
    c. propitiate : appease
    d. disperse : scatter
    e. abstain : invoke

UNIT S

Directions: Select the pair of words that most nearly expresses the relationship of the pair of key words in capital letters. Circle the letter preceding the pair you choose.

1. BARBER : RAZOR : :
   a. surgeon : scalpel
   b. chef : dinner
   c. teacher : book
   d. gymnast : exercise
   e. cowboy : gun

2. ADMIRAL : NAVY : :
   a. pilot : airplane
   b. general : army
   c. corporal : marines
   d. minister : congregation
   e. nurse : ward

3. DAMSEL : GIRL : :
   a. flapper : flirt
   b. ingenue : genius
   c. lad : boy
   d. stripling : parent
   e. stalk : vine

4. SYNDICATE : CORPORATION : :
   a. jamboree : regiment
   b. convention : meeting
   c. duet : trio
   d. period : punctuation
   e. dinner : banquet

5. MUNICIPAL : CITY : :
   a. federal : nation
   b. urbane : town
   c. judicial : court
   d. minute : hamlet
   e. nominal : state

6. SPATULA : TROWEL : :
   a. knife : scabbard
   b. gun : bullet
   c. rake : lawnmower
   d. ship : boat
   e. pitchfork : trident

7. HYPOTHESIS : THEORY : :
   a. eulogy : disparagement
   b. pulchritude : beauty
   c. lampoon : praise
   d. irony : strength
   e. lethargy : activity

8. EXCURSION : ODYSSEY : :
   a. hike : stroll
   b. voyage : journey
   c. dash : marathon
   d. trek : walk
   e. hurdle : race

9. SMALL : MINISCULE : :
   a. major : minor
   b. arid : dry
   c. momentous : trivial
   d. gigantic : large
   e. morose : sad

10. REPULSIVE : ODIOUS : :
    a. theoretical : certain
    b. abstract : withdrawn
    c. critical : bitter
    d. indigenous : primitive
    e. precarious : risky

11. AMELIORATE : LESSEN : :
    a. mangle : disturb
    b. enhance : charm
    c. augment : add
    d. desecrate : splatter
    e. squash : modify

12. TUNDRA : FROZEN : :
    a. jungle : inhabited
    b. ocean : wavy
    c. valley : eroded
    d. desert : arid
    e. pavement : durable

13. DEBACLE : DOWNFALL : :
    a. triumph : victory
    b. pillar : column
    c. fiasco : defeat
    d. skirmish : battle
    e. hurricane : storm

14. CUDGEL : STICK : :
    a. pebble : stone
    b. grain : sand
    c. cannon : rifle
    d. boulder : mountain
    e. tube : tire

15. IMPROVIDENT : BANKRUPTCY : :
    a. abundant : foliage
    b. affluent : laborer
    c. penurious : wealth
    d. destitute : thespian
    e. indigent : native

16. IDOL : ADULATION : :
    a. substitute : confidence
    b. puritan : praise
    c. celebrity : admiration
    d. scapegoat : blame
    e. host : affluence

17. SALVO : BARRAGE : :
    a. bedlam : pandemonium
    b. battle : war
    c. raucous : dulcet
    d. gun : cannon
    e. warship : fortress

18. COUNTERFEIT : BILL : :
    a. spurious : document
    b. complex : sentence
    c. intimate : letter
    d. descriptive : poem
    e. incomprehensible : ode

19. MAMMOTH : PRODIGIOUS : :
    a. infringe : violate
    b. gargantuan : colossal
    c. infinitesimal : titanic
    d. inane : foolish
    e. dinosaur : extinct

20. PATRON : MAGNANIMOUS : :
    a. recreant : trustworthy
    b. murderer : penitent
    c. plaintiff : legal
    d. oaf : voracious
    e. profligate : wasteful

UNIT T

Directions: Select the pair of words that most nearly expresses the relationship of the pair of key words in capital letters. Circle the letter preceding the pair you choose.

1. BIBLIOGRAPHY : TITLES : :
   a. manual : explanations
   b. atlas : margins
   c. lexicon : laws
   d. biography : truth
   e. gazetteer : facts

2. COMPOSER : CONDUCTOR : :
   a. producer : tragedy
   b. doctor : medicine
   c. trainer : coach
   d. lawyer : client
   e. playwright : director

3. MUMBLE : TALK : :
   a. scurry : scamper
   b. saunter : stride
   c. stagger : walk
   d. dream : sleep
   e. nap : doze

4. SPILL : POUR : :
   a. deceive : perjure
   b. dive : fall
   c. misstate : lie
   d. attack : charge
   e. sing : talk

5. CAVERN : CAVE : :
   a. library : bookshelf
   b. valley : gulch
   c. trunk : drawer
   d. hat : cap
   e. captain : sailor

6. GAUNT : EMACIATED : :
   a. hirsute : hairy
   b. buxom : obese
   c. fall : plunge
   d. stocky : portly
   e. slender : corpulent

7. MOURNER : DOLOROUS : :
   a. survivor : alive
   b. sojourner : restless
   c. vigilante : prudent
   d. victor : elated
   e. heir : related

8. TRITE : BANAL : :
   a. flawed : marred
   b. surreptitious : climactic
   c. overt : hidden
   d. threadbare : fashionable
   e. porous : moist

9. CLEAR : ENUNCIATE : :
   a. secret : whisper
   b. indistinct : stammer
   c. threaten : shout
   d. coherent : grunt
   e. convincing : gesticulate

10. EMBER : SMOLDER : :
    a. log : burn
    b. glass : shatter
    c. stone : tumble
    d. holocaust : destroy
    e. fire : rage

11. DECEPTION : ROGUE : :
    a. treason : traitor
    b. hope : pessimist
    c. law : anarchist
    d. democracy : monarchist
    e. espionage : spy

12. LOATHE : VILLAIN : :
    a. conciliate : counsel
    b. shun : cohort
    c. pity : recluse
    d. obliterate : building
    e. admire : paragon

13. POIGNANT : DRAMA : :
    a. popular : comedy
    b. hilarious : farce
    c. pungent : aroma
    d. inevitable : tragedy
    e. exciting : climax

14. TRANSITORY : PERMANENT : :
    a. hirsute : innocuous
    b. specious : counterfeit
    c. pensive : thoughtful
    d. sentimental : romantic
    e. callous : emotional

15. SPATULA : ICING : :
    a. hammer : nails
    b. trowel : mortar
    c. rake : leaves
    d. mop : water
    e. wrench : bolts

16. MOURNER : MELANCHOLY : :
    a. scion : apprehensive
    b. bungler : maladroit
    c. turncoat : fashionable
    d. malcontent : awkward
    e. sibling : jealous

17. DENOUNCE : INVEIGH : :
    a. dissent : quarrel
    b. construe : interpret
    c. countermand : revoke
    d. disseminate : scatter
    e. plaintiff : defendant

18. LARYNGITIS : SPEECH : :
    a. melancholia : heart
    b. microbe : health
    c. leukemia : breathing
    d. myopia : vision
    e. doze : sleep

19. ENAMOR : LOVE : :
    a. demur : insist
    b. repudiate : acknowledge
    c. ameliorate : hate
    d. alienate : estrange
    e. corroborate : confirm

20. INDUBITABLE : FALLACIOUS : :
    a. ostentatious : Spartan
    b. zealous : ardent
    c. meandering : circular
    d. quizzical : puzzled
    e. innuendo : hint

VOCABULARY GROUP I

1. **acrimonious**—*(adj.)* marked by hard or biting sharpness, especially of words, manner, or disposition; bitter.

2. **ambiguous**—*(adj.)* doubtful or uncertain, especially from obscurity or indistinctness; inexplicable; capable of being understood in more than one way.

3. **bellicose**—*(adj.)* showing readiness to quarrel or fight.

4. **bovine**—*(adj.)* related to or resembling the ox or cow; both sluggish and patient.—*(n.)* an ox or closely related animal.

5. **bucolic**—*(adj.)* rustic, rural, pastoral.

6. **burgeon**—*(v.)* to put forth, to sprout.—*(n.)* a bud, a sprout.

7. **burnish**—*(v.)* to polish, to make shiny by rubbing.—*(n.)* a gloss or polish.

8. **cadaver**—*(n.)* a corpse or dead body, especially of a person.

9. **callow**—*(adj.)* undeveloped, inexperienced, immature.

10. **candid**—*(adj.)* sincere, honest, impartial.

11. **captious**—*(adj.)* intended to entrap or confuse; quibbling, carping, faultfinding.

12. **carp**—*(v.)* to talk in a peevish, grumbling or accusing way; to find fault pettily or unfairly; cavil.—*(n.)* a fresh water fish.

13. **castigate**—*(v.)* to punish, chastise, or rebuke.

14. **chagrin**—*(n.)* vexation, disappointment, mortification, embarrassment.

15. **chimerical**—*(adj.)* imaginary, fantastic, unreal, absurd, impossible.

16. **clandestine**—*(adj.)* secret, hidden, underhanded, surreptitious.

17. **cloistered**—*(adj.)* secluded; hidden from the world, usually religious seclusion.

18. **copse**—*(n.)* a thicket of small trees.

19. **corroborate**—*(v.)* to support with evidence or authority; to make more certain.

20. **crass**—*(adj.)* grossly stupid; dull; coarse, gross.

21. **cursory**—*(adj.)* superficial, passing rapidly over something without attention to detail.

22. **debacle**—*(n.)* an overthrow, a rout; a sudden great disaster; a breakdown or collapse.

23. **deciduous**—*(adj.)* shedding leaves annually; shedding antlers or insect wings.

24. **deleterious**—*(adj.)* harmful, injurious.

25. **dirge**—*(n.)* a lament with music, a funeral hymn.

26. **dupe**—*(v.)* to deceive, to cheat.—*(n.)* a person easily fooled.

27. **ecclesiastical**—*(adj.)* of the church, or relating to the organization of the church or clergy.

28. **elliptical**—*(adj.)* resembling an ellipse or flattened circle; *grammar:* having a word or words omitted without being unintelligible.

29. **enigma**—*(n.)* a perplexing statement, matter or person; a riddle.

30. **enjoin**—*(v.)* to order officially; to forbid or prohibit.

31. **ephemeral**—*(adj.)* lasting one day; short-lived, transitory.

32. **epicure**—*(n.)* a connoisseur of food and drink; a person devoted to luxury and sensuous pleasure.

33. **ethereal**—*(adj.)* referring to the upper regions of space; light, airy, delicate, celestial.

34. **fallow**—*(n.)* land plowed but not sowed.—*(adj.)* left uncultivated; when describing the mind, untrained, inactive.

35. **fealty**—*(n.)* the duty and loyalty owed by a vassal to his lord—mostly used poetically in modern language.

36. **fetid**—*(adj.)* stinking, foully odorous.

37. **forensic**—*(adj.)* characteristic of or suitable for a law court or public debate; referring to a lawyer skilled in this area.

38. **fortuitous**—*(adj.)* happening by chance, accidental; lucky.

39. **frugal**—*(adj.)* not wasteful, thrifty.

40. **gargoyle**—(n.) a waterspout or ornament in the form of a carved animal—sometimes an imaginary one—projecting from the gutter of a building.

41. **gourmand**—(n.) a lover of good food; a glutton. (It is important to distinguish between this word and *gourmet* which connotes one with a fine taste in food and drink.)

42. **harbinger**—(n.) a person or thing that comes before to announce what is to follow.—(v.) to announce.

43. **hyperbole**—(n.) exaggeration for effect, not meant to be taken literally.

44. **imperturbable**—(adj.) unable to be disturbed or excited; impassive.

45. **incognito**—(adv. or adj.) with true identity not revealed; under disguise, with an assumed name.—(n.) a person who is incognito.

46. **indigenous**—(adj.) native, growing or produced naturally in a country or region.

47. **insurgent**—(n.) a rebel, one who opposes authority.—(adj.) rebellious.

48. **iniquitous**—(adj.) unjust, wicked.

49. **jingo**—(n.) a person who boasts of his or her patriotism; one who favors an aggressive foreign policy.

50. **jocose**—(adj.) humorous, joking, facetious.

51. **jubilant**—(adj.) joyful and triumphant.

52. **knell**—(v.) to ring, especially for a death, funeral, or disaster; to toll; to summon, announce, or proclaim as if by a knell.—(n.) the slow solemn sounding of a bell; an omen or signal of sorrow or death; any deep mournful sound.

53. **laity**—(n.) all people not included in the clergy; all people not included in a given profession.

54. **liturgy**—(n.) the prescribed ritual for public worship in any of various Christian churches.

55. **madrigal**—(n.) a short poem which can be set to music; a song with parts for several voices.

56. **mandate**—(n.) an authoritative order or command; the wishes of constituents expressed to their legislature or representative.—(v.) to order a nation to govern a geographical area.

57. **mentor**—(n.) a wise and loyal advisor; a teacher.

58. **millenium**—(n.) a thousand, especially a thousand years.

59. **mime**—(n.) an ancient Greek or Roman farce; a clown.—(v.) to play a part with gestures not words.

60. **minx**—(n.) a pert and saucy girl.

61. **mull**—(v.) to grind; to cogitate or ponder; to heat, sweeten, and flavor with spice.

62. **munificent**—(adj.) bountiful, lavish, generous.

63. **muse**—(v.) to ponder; to meditate.

64. **nebulous**—(adj.) cloudy, misty, vague.

65. **nefarious**—(adj.) wrong, wicked, villainous.

66. **parable**—(n.) a simple story from which a moral lesson may be drawn.

67. **parochial**—(adj.) narrow, limited, provincial.

68. **parsimonious**—(adj.) miserly, stingy.

69. **patrician**—(n.) a member of the nobility.—(adj.) noble, aristocratic.

70. **persiflage**—(n.) light, frivolous, flippant style in speaking or writing; banter, raillery.

71. **piquant**—(adj.) agreeably pungent or stimulating to the taste.

72. **piscatorial**—(adj.) of fishes, fishing, or people who fish.

73. **piscine**—(adj.) of or resembling a fish.

74. **plebescite**—(n.) an expression of the people's will by direct ballot.

75. **pliable**—(adj.) easily bent or molded; easily influenced.

76. **prelate**—(n.) a high ranking ecclesiastic such as a bishop.

77. **propitious**—(adj.) favorably inclined, boding well, being of good omen or auspicious.

78. **prude**—(n.) a person who is overly modest or proper.

79. **punctilious**—*(adj.)* scrupulous, exact.

80. **quibble**—*(v.)* to argue evasively.—*(n.)* a petty evasion.

81. **quixotic**—*(adj.)* extravagantly chivalrous; impractical.

82. **rapacious**—*(adj.)* very grasping or greedy; living on prey.

83. **recant**—*(v.)* to renounce beliefs formerly held.

84. **renowned**—*(adj.)* a state of being widely acclaimed and highly honored, famous.

85. **Samaritan**—*(n.)* person who comes to the aid of another; a native of Samaria.

86. **satiate**—*(v.)* to gratify with more than enough.—*(adj.)* sufficient or more than enough.

87. **secular**—*(adj.)* of or belonging to the world; worldly, not religious or sacred.

88. **sedentary**—*(adj.)* characterized by sitting: *a sedentary task.*

89. **sedulous**—*(adj.)* diligent, persistent, hard working.

90. **soiree**—*(n.)* an evening party or gathering.

91. **solon**—*(n.)* a wise person, a law maker.

92. **specter** (American spelling) or **spectre** (British spelling) —*(n.)* a ghost or an apparition.

93. **stipend**—*(n.)* a tax, tribute, or regular payment like a salary or pension.

94. **stylus**—*(n.)* a needlelike writing device; a phonograph needle.

95. **succumb**—*(v.)* to yield to superior strength or force or overpowering appeal or desire; to cease to exist, die.

96. **symposium**—*(n.)* a formal meeting at which several speakers deliver short addresses on a topic or related topics; a collection of opinions on a subject; a discussion.

97. **talisman**—*(n.)* anything with magic power; a good luck charm.

98. **talon**—*(n.)* a claw.

99. **tether**—*(n.)* a rope or chain fastened to an animal.

100. **tonsorial**—*(adj.)* relating to a barber or a barber's work.

VOCABULARY GROUP II

1. **abrogate**—*(v.)* to repeal, to cancel; to do away with.

2. **abstinent**—*(adj.)* practicing abstinence or refraining from something like food or drink.

3. **accolade**—*(n.)* a ceremony to mark the recognition of special merit; a mark of acknowledgment like a reward.

4. **acronym**—*(n.)* a word formed from the first letters of other words: *MADD—Mothers Against Drunk Driving.*

5. **adulate**—*(v.)* to flatter.

6. **aesthetic**—*(adj.)* sensitive to beauty.

7. **agnostic**—*(n.)* a person who thinks it is impossible to know whether there is a God or a future life.

8. **altruism**—*(n.)* concern for the welfare of others.

9. **amorphous**—*(adj.)* shapeless.

10. **anachronism**—*(n.)* something occurring in the wrong time: *George Washington drove a red Cadillac.*

11. **artisan**—*(n.)* a skilled craftsperson.

12. **askew**—*(adj.)* not symmetrical, awry; not straight.

13. **belligerent**—*(adj.)* hostile.

14. **bumptious**—*(adj.)* arrogant; pushy.

15. **cantankerous**—*(adj.)* contentious, perverse, grouchy.

16. **cauldron**—*(n.)* a large kettle.

17. **charlatan**—*(n.)* an imposter, a fraud or pretender.

18. **churlish**—*(adj.)* surly, boorish, miserly, unmannerly.

19. **clement**—*(adj.)* lenient, merciful; mild—usually refers to the weather.

20. **construe**—*(v.)* to understand or explain the sense or orientation of; interpret.

21. **contrite**—*(adj.)* remorseful.

22. **convivial**—*(adj.)* sociable, jovial.

23. **corsair**—*(n.)* a privateer, a pirate; a pirate ship.

24. **coterie**—*(n.)* a group which gathers for social purposes; social circle, clique.

25. **crone**—*(n.)* a withered old woman.

26. **crypt**—*(n.)* an underground chamber, vault serving as burial place.

27. **diaphanous**—*(adj.)* delicate, transparent.

28. **disconcerting**—*(adj.)* upsetting, frustrating.

29. **dissonance**—*(n.)* a harsh or unpleasant sound or combination of sounds; lack of agreement, discord.

30. **docile**—*(adj.)* teachable, tractable.

31. **dolt**—*(n.)* a stupid, slow-witted person.

32. **denouement**—*(n.)* the outcome of a plot in a drama or story.

33. **dotard**—*(n.)* a person in his or her dotage or second childhood; a senile person.

34. **elucidate**—*(v.)* to make clear, to explain.

35. **emporium**—*(n.)* a trading center, a large store, a market place.

36. **entourage**—*(n.)* surroundings, environment; a group of attendants.

37. **estrange**—*(v.)* to remove; to turn away, to alienate.

38. **fervent**—*(adj.)* hot, burning, ardent.

39. **fiscal**—*(adj.)* having to do with public money, financial.

40. **florid**—*(adj.)* rosy, ruddy, highly colored.

41. **fractious**—*(adj.)* unruly, rebellious; peevish, fretful.

42. **gossamer**—*(n.)* a thin, filmy cloth.—*(adj.)* light, thin, filmy.

43. **gregarious**—*(adj.)* fond of company, sociable; living in herds or flocks.

44. **gustatory**—*(adj.)* pertaining to the sense of taste.

45. **hamlet**—*(n.)* a small group of houses in the country; in capitalized form, Shakespeare's Prince of Denmark.

46. **hedonism**—*(n.)* the doctrine that pleasure is the principal good and should be the aim of action.

47. **heinous**—*(adj.)* extremely wicked, abominable.

48. **homonym**—*(n.)* a word with the same pronunciation as another but with a different meaning and usually different spelling: *bore* and *boar.*

49. **hoyden**—*(n.)* a boisterous girl, a tomboy.—*(adj.)* tomboyish.

50. **imbibe**—*(v.)* to drink, to absorb.

51. **immolate**—*(v.)* to offer or kill, as a sacrifice.

52. **indigence**—*(n.)* poverty, neediness.

53. **ingenuous**—*(adj.)* showing innocent or childlike simplicity, naive.

54. **innundate**—*(v.)* to overflow, to flood.

55. **insidious**—*(adj.)* plotting treacherously; crafty, wily, lying in wait.

56. **irascible**—*(adj.)* easily angered, quick tempered.

57. **lethargic**—*(adj.)* abnormally drowsy, dull, sluggish.

58. **litigation**—*(n.)* the process of carrying on a lawsuit.

59. **lugubrious**—*(adj.)* mournful, dismal.

60. **malign**—*(v.)* to defame, to speak evil of.—*(adj.)* malevolent, malicious.

61. **malodorous**—*(adj.)* stinking.

62. **maraud**—*(v.)* to raid, plunder or pillage.—*(n.)* a raid, foray.

63. **minuscule**—*(adj.)* tiny, minute.

64. **mogul**—*(n.)* a powerful, important person.

65. **mottled**—*(adj.)* marked with blotches or spots.

66. **nonentity**—*(n.)* a person of little importance; the state of not existing.

67. **noxious**—*(adj.)* harmful to health or morals, unwholesome.

68. **oaf**—*(n.)* a stupid, clumsy fellow.

69. **obdurate**—*(adj.)* hard hearted, hardened.

70. **olfactory**—*(adj.)* of the sense of smell.

71. **pathology**—*(n.)* the branch of medicine that deals with the nature of disease; the conditions or results of a particular disease.

72. **pedant**—*(n.)* a narrow-minded teacher, a person who stresses unnecessarily minor or trivial points of learning.

73. **peregrinate**—*(v.)* to journey, travel.

74. **perfidious**—*(adj.)* treacherous.

75. **phalanx**—*(n.)* soldiers arranged in order for battle; a mass or group of individuals with a single common purpose.

76. **pique**—*(v.)* to arouse resentment.

77. **posterity**—*(n.)* all of a person's descendants.

78. **pragmatic**—*(adj.)* busy, active, practical.

79. **prevaricate**—*(v.)* to lie.

80. **progeny**—*(n.)* descendants, children; offspring of animals or plants.

81. **ravish**—*(v.)* to seize and take away by violence; to overcome with emotion; to rape; to plunder or rob.

82. **raze**—*(v.)* to level to the ground.

83. **recondite**—*(adj.)* profound, abstruse, obscure, concealed.

84. **remunerate**—*(v.)* to reward, recompense, pay.

85. **rill**—*(n.)* a little brook or river; a long narrow trench or valley on the moon's surface.

86. **sagacious**—*(adj.)* wise, shrewd.

87. **sequester**—*(v.)* to set apart, separate.

88. **spate**—*(n.)* a flooded condition; an unusually large outpouring.

89. **strident**—*(adj.)* harsh sounding.

90. **sychophant**—*(n.)* a servile self-serving flatterer; parasite.

91. **synod**—*(n.)* a council of churches or church officials.

92. **truculent**—*(adj.)* fierce, savage, cruel.

93. **tycoon**—*(n.)* a business executive of exceptional wealth and power; a top leader (as in politics).

94. **tyro**—*(n.)* a beginner.

95. **upbraid**—*(v.)* to criticize or scold severely or vehemently.

96. **viaduct**—*(n.)* a long bridge that carries a road.

97. **virulent**—*(adj.)* deadly; bitterly hostile.

98. **vituperative**—*(adj.)* abusive.

99. **vulpine**—*(adj.)* clever, cunning, tricky like a fox.

100. **wizened**—*(adj.)* dried, shriveled, and wrinkled especially with age.

VOCABULARY GROUP III

1. **adage**—*(n.)* a traditional saying expressing a common experience or observation; a proverb.

2. **allegation**—*(n.)* an assertion made as if it were a fact.

3. **anthropology**—*(n.)* the study of people—customs, origin, distribution, and social and environmental relations.

4. **aperture**—*(n.)* an opening, hole, gap.

5. **apiary**—*(n.)* a place where bees are kept.

6. **arraign**—*(v.)* to charge with guilt.

7. **atrium**—*(n.)* the central court of an ancient Roman house.

8. **aversion**—*(n.)* an intense or definite dislike, antipathy.

9. **aviary**—*(n.)* a large cage housing many birds.

10. **banal**—*(adj.)* lacking originality, trite, hackneyed.

11. **bastion**—*(n.)* any strong defense or bulwark, fortress.

12. **behemoth**—*(n.)* a huge animal.

13. **boor**—*(n.)* a rude, ill-mannered person.

14. **bowdlerize**—*(v.)* to expurgate; to remove obscenity from a book.

15. **cacophony**—*(n.)* a harsh jarring sound, discord.

16. **censure**—*(n.)* a blaming adverse opinion or judgment.—*(v.)* to criticize as blameworthy.

17. **citadel**—*(n.)* a fortress on a commanding height.

18. **concordance**—*(n.)* agreement, harmony.

19. **condiment**—*(n.)* something used to enhance the flavor of food; a spice.

20. **confluence**—*(n.)* a flowing together of two streams.

21. **congenital**—*(adj.)* resulting from heredity, innate, existing at birth.

22. **coquette**—*(n.)* a girl who flirts.

23. **crony**—*(n.)* a familiar friend, close companion.

24. **cudgel**—*(n.)* a thick stick or club.—*(v.)* to beat with a cudgel.

25. **cupola**—*(n.)* a rounded roof or ceiling; a small dome on a roof; a small furnace for melting metals; a revolving gun turret.

26. **curator**—*(n.)* the guardian of a minor; a person in charge of a museum.

27. **cynical**—*(adj.)* scornfully distrustful of human nature or motives.

28. **dastard**—*(n.)* a mean, skulking coward.

29. **debit**—*(n.)* a record of indebtedness; a drawback or shortcoming.—*(v.)* to enter on the left-hand side of an account.

30. **dowager**—*(n.)* a widow holding property or a title from her deceased husband; a dignified elderly woman.

31. **effusive**—*(adj.)* pouring out, overflowing, too demonstrative.

32. **epigram**—*(n.)* a short poem with a witty point; any terse, witty, pointed statement.

33. **etymology**—*(n.)* the origin or history of a word: *"Etymology" comes from the Greek word "etymologia."*

34. **eulogize**—*(v.)* to praise highly.

35. **euphony**—*(n.)* a pleasing sound, often a combination of sounds as in music.

36. **exacerbate**—*(v.)* to exasperate; to make angry, aggravate, irritate.

37. **expurgate**—*(v.)* to purge.

38. **extemporize**—*(v.)* to improvise.

39. **exuberant**—*(adj.)* joyously unrestrained, luxuriant, prolific.

40. **exult**—*(v.)* to rejoice greatly, to be jubilant.

41. **felicitous**—*(adj.)* appropriate, aptly chosen.

42. **felon**—*(n.)* a person guilty of a major crime; a painful infection at the end of a finger or toe.

43. **fiduciary**—*(adj.)* having the relationship of a trustee: *a fiduciary guardian of a minor child.*

44. **fleet**—*(n.)* a number of warships or other ships under one control.—*(adv.)* fast, speedy.

45. **fruition**—*(n.)* a coming to fulfillment, a realization.

46. **gibberish**—*(n.)* rapid incoherent language.

47. **gibe**—*(v.)* to jeer, taunt, or sneer.

48. **Herculean**—*(adj.)* having great size and strength like Hercules in Greek mythology.

49. **hovel**—*(n.)* any small miserable dwelling.

50. **impeach**—*(v.)* to bring an accusation against; to charge before a tribunal with misconduct in office.

51. **intrepid**—*(adj.)* unafraid.

52. **jabber**—*(v.)* to speak incoherently, chatter, gibber.—*(n.)* incoherent talk.

53. **lampoon**—*(n.)* a harsh satire directed against an individual or institution.—*(v.)* to ridicule.

54. **lassitude**—*(n.)* a feeling of being tired or weak.

55. **lionize**—*(v.)* to treat as a celebrity.

56. **magnanimous**—*(adj.)* noble in mind; generous in overlooking insult.

57. **malefactor**—*(n.)* a criminal.

58. **martinet**—*(n.)* a strict disciplinarian.

59. **maudlin**—*(adj.)* foolishly tearful, weakly sentimental.

60. **maxim**—*(n.)* a concisely expressed principle; a proverb.

61. **mendacity**—*(n.)* a lie or falsehood.

62. **mendicant**—*(n.)* a beggar.

63. **misanthrope**—*(n.)* a person who hates all people.

64. **misogyny**—*(n.)* hatred of women.

65. **mutable**—*(adj.)* capable of change or of being changed.

66. **neophyte**—*(n.)* a new convert; any beginner.

67. **niggardly**—*(adj.)* stingy, miserly.

68. **noisome**—*(adj.)* noxious, harmful, foul smelling.

69. **numismatics**—*(n.)* the study of coins.

70. **obsequious**—*(adj.)* overly submissive, fawning.

71. **obtuse**—*(adj.)* blunt, dull; an angle that is greater than 90°.

72. **paragon**—*(n.)* a model of perfection; a perfect diamond of 100 carats or more.

73. **pariah**—*(n.)* any outcast despised by others.

74. **penury**—*(n.)* poverty, destitution.

75. **philatelist**—*(n.)* a stamp collector.

76. **philologist**—*(n.)* one who studies written records; one who studies literature or language as it is used in literature.

77. **platitude**—*(n.)* flatness, dullness; a trite remark.

78. **pommel**—*(v.)* to beat.—*(n.)* the rounded projection on the front of a saddle; the round knob on the end of a sword.

79. **potentate**—*(n.)* a ruler or monarch.

80. **predilection**—*(n.)* a preconceived liking, partiality, preference.

81. **prodigal**—*(adj.)* extremely generous; wasteful.

82. **prognosis**—*(n.)* a forecasting of the probable course and termination of a disease.

83. **protagonist**—*(n.)* the main character in a story.

84. **renegade**—*(n.)* a traitor, turncoat, deserter.

85. **retinue**—*(n.)* an escorting group; a group of people in service of another.

86. **sage**—*(n.)* a wise person; a plant of the mint family.—*(adj.)* wise, perceptive, discerning.

87. **scurrilous**—*(adj.)* using coarse language, being vulgar and evil.

88. **servile**—*(adj.)* cringing; humbly yielding or submissive.

89. **siren**—*(n.)* in Greek mythology a nymph who lured sailors to death by singing; a warning signal, a whistle; a small lizard-shaped animal.—*(adj.)* of or like a siren; seductive, tempting.

90. **slatternly**—*(adj.)* like an untidy person; like a slut.

91. **sobriquet**—*(n.)* a nickname; an assumed name.

92. **soporific**—*(adj.)* causing sleep; dull.

93. **squalid**—*(adj.)* foul, unclean, sordid.

94. **taciturn**—*(adj.)* uncommunicative.

95. **tautology**—*(n.)* needless repetition of an idea, statement or word.

96. **tempestuous**—*(adj.)* violent, turbulent.

97. **titanic**—*(adj.)* of great size; designating a chemical compound containing titanium.

98. **translucent**—*(adj.)* partially transparent, like frosted glass.

99. **turbulent**—*(adj.)* unruly, boisterous, tumultuous.

100. **virtuoso**—*(n.)* a person who has special knowledge or skill in a field; a person who excels in musical technique or execution.

VOCABULARY GROUP IV

1. **accede**—(v.) to consent, to agree.

2. **adulation**—(n.) excessive praise or flattery.

3. **agile**—(adj.) quick, deft, active.

4. **ameliorate**—(v.) to make better or improve.

5. **amiable**—(adj.) friendly, pleasant.

6. **archipelago**—(n.) a group of islands; any sea with many islands.

7. **assiduous**—(adj.) diligent, hard-working, persevering.

8. **atrophy**—(v.) to waste away; to fail to grow.

9. **avarice**—(n.) greed for riches, cupidity.

10. **bedecked**—(adj.) adorned.

11. **benign**—(adj.) favorable; beneficial; of mild character.

12. **besotted**—(adj.) silly, foolish.

13. **bevy**—(n.) a group of girls or women; a flock; a collection of objects.

14. **blithe**—(adj.) gay, joyful, cheerful.

15. **brigand**—(n.) a bandit.

16. **brusque**—(adj.) blunt, short in manner.

17. **chauvinist**—(n.) a person unreasonably devoted to his own race, sex, etc

18. **cogitate**—(v.) to think seriously.

19. **cohort**—(n.) a Roman military unit making up one tenth of a legion; a group, a band of people.

20. **conjugal**—(adj.) matrimonial, connubial.

21. **construe**—(v.) to explain; to deduce or interpret; to analyze a clause or sentence to show its grammatical construction.

22. **contiguous**—(adj.) touching, near, adjoining, abutting.

23. **corpulent**—(adj.) fat, stout, obese.

24. **countermand**—(v.) to recall or order back by a contrary order.

25. **coxswain**—(n.) a person who steers a boat or racing shell and usually has charge of a crew.

26. **craven**—(adj.) cowardly.— (n.) a coward.

27. **crescendo**—(n.) a gradual increase in loudness of music: *a passage played crescendo.*

28. **cryptic**—(adj.) secret; intended to be obscure or mysterious.

29. **debut**—(n.) a first appearance; a formal entrance into society.

30. **demur**—(v.) to hesitate; to take exception to, to disagree.

31. **desecrate**—(v.) to treat as not sacred, to profane.

32. **diffident**—(adj.) shy.

33. **disgruntled**—(adj.) discontented, in bad humor.

34. **disseminate**—(v.) to scatter widely, to spread abroad.

35. **dolorous**—(adj.) sad, painful, mournful.

36. **dulcet**—(adj.) soothing, pleasant, melodious.

37. **edify**—(v.) to instruct; to improve morally or spiritually.

38. **epaulet**—(n.) a shoulder ornament on a uniform.

39. **epitaph**—(n.) an inscription on a tomb.

40. **epithet**—(n.) an adjective, noun, or phrase considered characteristic of a person or thing.

41. **espouse**—(v.) to marry.

42. **euphemism**—(n.) a word or phrase considered less distasteful than another.

43. **fastidious**—(adj.) very critical; over sensitive.

44. **furtive**—(adj.) surreptitious, sly, shifty.

45. **gargantuan**—(adj.) huge.

46. **gauntlet**—(n.) a medieval glove; a long glove with a flaring cuff.

47. **glossary**—(n.) a list of foreign, difficult, or technical terms.

48. **hirsute**—(adj.) hairy, bristly.

49. **improvident**—(adj.) not providing for the future; rash.

50. **inane**—(adj.) foolish, silly, empty.

51. **incandescent**—(adj.) very bright, gleaming.

52. **indigent**—(adj.) poor, needy, destitute.

53. **insipid**—(adj.) tasteless, dull, lifeless.

54. **kleptomaniac**—*(n.)* a person with an abnormal impulse to steal.

55. **laconic**—*(adj.)* using a minimum of words; concise to the point of seeming rude or mysterious.

56. **lexicon**—*(n.)* a dictionary.

57. **Lilliputian**—*(adj.)* tiny, very small.

58. **maladroit**—*(adj.)* awkward, clumsy.

59. **matriculate**—*(v.)* to enroll as a student or candidate.

60. **medley**—*(n.)* a mixture; a piece of music made up of parts of other musical pieces.

61. **meticulous**—*(adj.)* excessively careful about details.

62. **motley**—*(adj.)* of many colors.—*(n.)* a mixture of things that are different.

63. **mundane**—*(adj.)* worldly, earthly.

64. **myopic**—*(adj.)* nearsighted, unable to see clearly.

65. **nomenclature**—*(n.)* a name or designation; a system of terms used in a particular science, discipline, or art.

66. **ostentatious**—*(adj.)* showy, pretentious.

67. **overt**—*(adj.)* open, public, observable.

68. **perfunctory**—*(adj.)* done without care or interest.

69. **plebian**—*(n.)* a vulgar, coarse person; a common person.

70. **poignant**—*(adj.)* sharp or biting to taste; sharply painful to the feelings, keen.

71. **precarious**—*(adj.)* uncertain, insecure.

72. **prodigious**—*(adj.)* impressively great in size, force, or extent; enormous, extraordinary.

73. **prolix**—*(adj.)* wordy to a tiresome degree.

74. **propitiate**—*(v.)* to cause to be favorably inclined; to appease or conciliate.

75. **prudent**—*(adj.)* cautious, discreet.

76. **pulchritude**—*(n.)* physical beauty.

77. **quell**—*(v.)* to crush, subdue, quiet, allay.

78. **raucous**—*(adj.)* hoarse, rough sounding.

79. **recreant**—*(n.)* a coward, a craven.—*(adj.)* craven, cowardly.

80. **redress**—*(n.)* correction; compensation.—*(v.)* to correct or remedy.

81. **rhetorical**—*(adj.)* relating to the art of speaking or writing.

82. **rogue**—*(n.)* a tramp; a rascal; a fun-loving, mischievous person.

83. **salubrious**—*(adj.)* wholesome, healthy.

84. **salvo**—*(n.)* a discharge of artillery as a salute.

85. **sanctuary**—*(n.)* a place of refuge or protection; a holy place.

86. **slovenly**—*(adj.)* careless, untidy, slipshod.

87. **spatula**—*(n.)* a flat-bladed tool used for spreading.

88. **specious**—*(adj.)* seeming to be good without being so; not genuine.

89. **spurious**—*(adj.)* false.

90. **stripling**—*(n.)* an immature young person, a youth.

91. **thespian**—*(n.)* an actor or actress.

92. **tundra**—*(n.)* treeless plains in the Arctic.

93. **urbane**—*(adj.)* polite, suave, sophisticated.

94. **usurp**—*(v.)* to assume power by force.

95. **verbose**—*(adj.)* wordy, long-winded.

96. **verdant**—*(adj.)* green.

97. **vignette**—*(n.)* a very short literary composition.

98. **vixen**—*(n.)* a bad-tempered woman; a female fox.

99. **voluble**—*(adj.)* wordy, talkative.

100. **zealot**—*(n.)* fanatic; someone who is excessively enthusiastic.

ANSWERS FOR THE ANALOGY GROUPS

Group I

Unit A	Unit B	Unit C	Unit D	Unit E
1. d	1. c	1. b	1. b	1. e
2. b	2. b	2. e	2. d	2. d
3. c	3. e	3. c	3. e	3. e
4. e	4. c	4. b	4. b	4. c
5. a	5. d	5. d	5. c	5. e
6. d	6. e	6. c	6. e	6. c
7. a	7. e	7. b	7. d	7. d
8. d	8. e	8. e	8. c	8. d
9. d	9. a	9. e	9. b	9. c
10. e	10. d	10. b	10. a	10. b
11. b	11. a	11. c	11. b	11. e
12. a	12. d	12. c	12. a	12. d
13. b	13. b	13. a	13. b	13. e
14. d	14. e	14. b	14. c	14. c
15. c	15. c	15. d	15. c	15. d
16. d	16. e	16. a	16. d	16. c
17. e	17. b	17. b	17. c	17. e
18. b	18. b	18. d	18. b	18. a
19. e	19. e	19. a	19. e	19. e
20. d	20. c	20. a	20. d	20. d

Group II

Unit F	Unit G	Unit H	Unit I	Unit J
1. b	1. c	1. b	1. c	1. e
2. c	2. b	2. b	2. a	2. b
3. b	3. e	3. e	3. d	3. b
4. d	4. b	4. e	4. a	4. a
5. a	5. b	5. b	5. e	5. c
6. c	6. c	6. c	6. b	6. b
7. a	7. c	7. a	7. c	7. c
8. b	8. b	8. c	8. b	8. c
9. e	9. a	9. c	9. a	9. e
10. c	10. e	10. b	10. b	10. e
11. a	11. b	11. e	11. e	11. d
12. e	12. d	12. b	12. d	12. b
13. c	13. e	13. e	13. e	13. c
14. e	14. b	14. c	14. c	14. e
15. b	15. c	15. d	15. e	15. b
16. d	16. a	16. b	16. e	16. b
17. c	17. b	17. c	17. c	17. a
18. b	18. e	18. e	18. b	18. b
19. a	19. e	19. b	19. a	19. c
20. b	20. d	20. d	20. b	20. e

Group III

Unit K	Unit L	Unit M	Unit N	Unit O
1. b	1. a	1. d	1. b	1. d
2. b	2. e	2. c	2. e	2. b
3. c	3. e	3. c	3. e	3. e
4. a	4. b	4. e	4. a	4. a
5. a	5. b	5. b	5. b	5. c
6. e	6. c	6. d	6. e	6. b
7. e	7. e	7. a	7. e	7. e
8. c	8. d	8. a	8. c	8. d
9. e	9. b	9. c	9. b	9. b
10. a	10. c	10. e	10. e	10. e
11. e	11. b	11. e	11. d	11. d
12. e	12. c	12. b	12. a	12. b
13. d	13. b	13. b	13. b	13. b
14. c	14. d	14. b	14. e	14. c
15. e	15. d	15. a	15. d	15. b
16. b	16. a	16. b	16. d	16. c
17. c	17. b	17. d	17. e	17. a
18. a	18. e	18. a	18. c	18. c
19. b	19. e	19. c	19. c	19. e
20. e	20. e	20. d	20. b	20. a

Group IV

Unit P	Unit Q	Unit R	Unit S	Unit T
1. d	1. c	1. b	1. a	1. e
2. e	2. b	2. b	2. b	2. e
3. a	3. b	3. a	3. c	3. c
4. b	4. a	4. b	4. b	4. c
5. a	5. e	5. e	5. a	5. b
6. b	6. a	6. d	6. e	6. b
7. e	7. e	7. b	7. b	7. d
8. a	8. c	8. c	8. c	8. a
9. e	9. e	9. e	9. d	9. b
10. b	10. e	10. a	10. e	10. a
11. a	11. d	11. d	11. c	11. a
12. c	12. e	12. a	12. d	12. e
13. e	13. c	13. c	13. c	13. b
14. d	14. d	14. e	14. c	14. e
15. c	15. b	15. a	15. c	15. b
16. e	16. e	16. d	16. d	16. b
17. c	17. d	17. c	17. a	17. a
18. b	18. c	18. b	18. a	18. d
19. e	19. e	19. b	19. b	19. d
20. c	20. b	20. c	20. e	20. a